JERSEY WAR WALKS

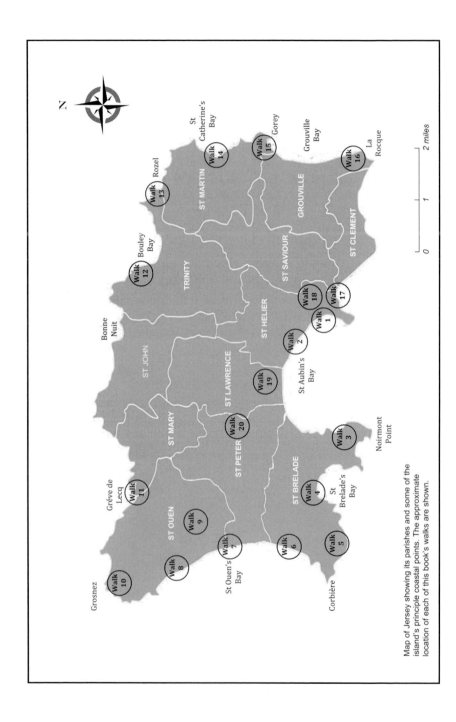

Map of Jersey showing its parishes and some of the island's principle coastal points. The approximate location of each of this book's walks are shown.

JERSEY
WAR
WALKS

~ Exploring the fortified isle ~

Ian Ronayne

SEAFLOWER BOOKS

Published in 2012
Reprinted with revisions in 2016
by SEAFLOWER BOOKS
11 Regents Place
Bradford on Avon
Wiltshire   BA15 1ED

Origination by Seaflower Books
www.ex-librisbooks.co.uk

Printed by CPI Anthony Rowe
Chippenham, Wiltshire

ISBN 978-1-906641-44-3

*For my father, who first opened my eyes to
the history and beauty that surrounds us*

Contents

Introduction

Walk anywhere in Jersey and it is impossible not to come across evidence of the island's remarkable military past. Reminders abound, fashioned from stone, concrete and metal, with some intact and fully recognisable while others lie ruined or half-buried. Many are clustered together at key locations, or seemingly piled on top of one another, making it difficult to decipher the period that they belong to, or the purpose for which they were built. The fact that many are found along Jersey's coastline is no coincidence of course; but what a fortunate coincidence that results in a combination of breathtaking scenery, charming walks and fascinating military history.

Jersey's military history and its fortifications have always fascinated me, both the well-known aspects and popular sites and the more obscure stories and locations. One cause of irritation, however, has been a tendency for literature or guides to focus on just one period or subject, minimising or even ignoring the multi-layered historical fabric that actually exists. So the twenty walks chosen for this book encompass all periods and aspects of Jersey's military history, from the Iron Age to the Occupation, as they are discovered in passing. The book does not attempt to cover every element of Jersey's military history or fortifications however – in fact, there are some interesting and important parts missing. It was more essential to ensure the walks follow logical routes with a good balance of exercise, scenery and points of interest while trying to avoid busy roads or hazardous thoroughfares. One regret is that space limitations meant leaving out any reference to non-military subjects, although here and there they squeeze their way in.

For each walk, there is a length in miles and estimate of time taken together with a guide to the effort required, although of course everyone's pace and stamina is different. Each also suggests options for getting to the walk's start, although readers should bear in mind car-parking arrangements change, as do bus timetables and availability, especially in winter. A guide to refreshment options and amenities en route is included, but in the briefest terms.

Finally, this is not a history book, or an academic study of Jersey's military past and fortifications -– other publications exist to serve that purpose far better, and should be consulted by anyone wanting to find out more. It is a book for people who enjoy walking, and who would like to understand more about the military history landscape through which they are passing. I hope you enjoy reading and using the book as much as I have enjoyed writing it.

Ian Ronayne
Jersey
May 2012

Jersey's military history and fortifications: a brief account

While this book is not intended as an account of Jersey's rich and varied military history, readers may find the following brief account useful in helping place fortifications and locations in context when visiting them.

Iron Age to Dark Ages

Little is known about the people living in Jersey around three thousand years ago during the Iron Age, or the society in which they existed. They had reason to defend themselves, however, and thus build the earliest fortifications still visible in the island today at Grève de Lecq and above Rozel. While there may be questions over the origins and purpose of Le Câtel de Lecq and Le Câtel de Rozel, indications are they were Iron Age promontory forts, similar to those found in Ireland and Cornwall. There is certainly compelling evidence to suggest an Iron Age fort once stood on the site later occupied by Mont Orgueil Castle, and there may have been other similar fortifications lost with the passing of time.

As to the fate of Jersey and its inhabitants during the five hundred years when the Romans ruled this part of Europe, and during the Dark Ages that followed, only scant evidence exists, although in common with other regions, Jersey would have experienced Viking raids and settlement. The story of the island really comes into recorded history in 933, when William Longsword, the Duke of Normandy, made Jersey part of his expanding dominion. As a result, men from Jersey may have accompanied Duke William to Hastings in 1066, taking part in the fateful battle there that sealed his reputation as conqueror and added the crown of England to his other titles. William's conquest left Jersey at the quiet heart of a realm encompassing both sides of the Channel, far from dangerous frontiers. Everything changed in 1204, however, when a power struggle following the death of Richard Lionheart led to Normandy becoming part of the Kingdom of France.

The Medieval and Tudor Periods

Following 1204, Richard's brother John was determined to hold onto the Channel Islands, then the last outpost of his Norman lands. He ordered their garrisoning and the construction of a powerful fortification to guard Jersey's now vulnerable east coast. The building of Mont Orgueil Castle marked the start of over 600 years of hostile rivalry between England and France, and numerous wars and conflicts that placed Jersey firmly in the front line.

For the next three centuries, the island was subject to attacks and invasions by French forces keen to remove this troublesome English stronghold. During most, Mont Orgueil Castle held out until the invaders either left or an English relieving force arrived, although it did fall into French hands between 1461 and 1468. Other raiders visited the island from time to time, including a force in 1406 led by Castilian nobleman Pero Niño, who narrowly defeated the island's defenders on the sands outside St Helier. During these invasions and raids, the population often sought shelter in some of the island's other fortifications of this period, including Grosnez Castle at Les Landes, and a large earthwork construction known as Castel Sedement or Les Câtieaux in Trinity.

Among the defenders standing against these invaders were men of the Jersey Militia. Although the militia's exact origins are uncertain, from the time of King John at least there appears to have been an organised force of local soldiers summoned to arms in the event of an attack on the island. By 1545, the arrangement had become more formal, with each of the Island's twelve parishes contributing a 'Trained Band', and possessing two pieces of artillery of the type seen today near the bottom of Beaumont Hill. In 1549, they proved their worth by defeating a French force that landed in Bouley Bay.

By the late 15th century, while the threat from France remained as strong as ever, the evolution of military technology had put the future of Mont Orgueil in doubt. Although it could withstand the arrows of earlier times, cannon placed on the nearby Mont St Nicolas could increasingly dominate the castle. As a result, there was a comprehensive remodelling undertaken from the 1460s onwards, both to protect against cannon fire and to mount cannon to hit back. While this work, which created the fortification seen today, managed to extend the castle's life, it could not ultimately save it from obsolescence, which was finally admitted at the end of the 16th century with the building of new fortification on an islet off the increasingly important settlement in St Helier.

The south of the island already had one fortification at this time, a tower and battery built between 1542 and 1545 on the islet outside St Aubin to defend Jersey's then principal port and place of commerce. The growing importance of St Helier led to the construction of a more powerful fortress on the opposite side of the bay, however, named Elizabeth Castle in honour of the then reigning monarch. Prior to this, the only building on the islet was a priory founded to honour the memory of Saint Helier, reputedly killed on the spot by pirates in AD555. The new castle was built in phases, slowly increasing in size and complexity during the 17th century to take the form that exists today. Ironically, however, the first substantial challenge to this new fortification would come not from the French, but an English army.

The English Civil War

At the start of the English Civil War, the island was under the control Sir Philip De Carteret, Seigneur of St Ouen's Manor and head of Jersey's most powerful dynasty. In 1643, dismayed at his neutral stance, a Parliamentarian delegation arrived and with the help of sympathetic islanders removed Sir Philip, who took refuge in Elizabeth Castle. Shortly thereafter, his nephew George Carteret, who was an ardent Royalist, seized control and held Jersey for the King. He strongly fortified the island, preparing both Mont Orgueil and Elizabeth Castles for war, and sent privateers to attack Parliamentarian ships in the Channel. In 1646, with the war in Britain turning against the Royalists, the King's son, the future Charles II, sought refuge in Jersey before fleeing to France, and returned again briefly in 1649, when he was declared King following the execution of his father. Despite what appeared to be a lost cause, Carteret continued to harry Parliamentarian ships with Jersey-based vessels, and so, in 1651, Britain's new government decided to remove the threat once and for all.

In October that year, a Parliamentarian fleet arrived off Jersey, landing a force in St Ouen's Bay. Although George Carteret initially resisted, the less enthusiastic militiamen under his command soon melted away and he fled to Elizabeth Castle. Despite Mont Orgueil quickly surrendering, Carteret prepared for a long siege, believing Elizabeth Castle impregnable due to its offshore location. But a mortar shell fired from a powerful Parliamentarian battery located near what is today Pier Road hit the castle's ammunition store in the old priory, killing a number of men and shocking the garrison towards the negotiating table. On 12 December 1651, Elizabeth Castle surrendered, ending the Civil War in Jersey.

The Battle of Jersey

The years following the English Civil War saw a reorganisation of Jersey's defences. While regular British soldiers continued to garrison the castles, the Jersey Militia, by now clad in the famous British redcoat, became increasingly important, being organised in 1730 into five regiments. The 1st or North-West Regiment represented the parishes of St Ouen, St Mary and St John, the 2nd or North Regiment those of Trinity and St Martin, while the 3rd or East Regiment recruited men from St Saviour, Grouville and St Clement. The 4th or South Regiment drew its men from the most populous parishes of St Helier and St Lawrence, being the only one possessing two battalions as a result. Finally, the 5th or South-West Regiment took its men from the parishes of St Peter and St Brelade. Supporting these infantry units were the militia artillery, whose cannon were kept in the parish churches, and a unit of cavalry. Every male between the ages of 15 and 65 were bound to serve, giving the island a trained force of around three thousand men.

Complementing the reorganised human component of the island's defences was a development of smaller fortifications consisting mainly of cannon batteries around Jersey's coast, with the landing in St Ouen's Bay during the Civil War showing how vulnerable the island was to invasion. In 1779, the reorganised defences were put to the test when the French under the Prince of Nassau attempted to land in St Ouen's Bay, but were repulsed by a force of regular army and militia. The event was a wake-up call, although by then the island's governor, General Henry Conway, had already set in motion a plan to improve the coastal defences. Conway planned to build 30 towers of a design unique to Jersey at key locations around the island, to be manned by the infantry of the militia and with a single cannon on top capable of all round fire. Although only 22 of these Conway-style round towers were actually completed, the last being La Rocco Tower in St Ouen's Bay, most remain to this day as distinctive reminders of his ambitious plans. Unfortunately for Conway, his efforts started too late to prevent an invasion that for a while appeared to have lost Jersey to France.

On the night of 6 January 1781, a small force of French soldiers under the command of Baron De Rullecourt landed at La Rocque and marched towards St Helier without encountering resistance. Surprising the lieutenant-governor, Moses Corbett, in his bed, they obtained the island's capitulation by exaggerating the size of the invading army and threatening to destroy the town. Unfortunately for De Rullecourt, both the defenders of Elizabeth Castle, led by Captain Mulcaster, and the commander of the British regular troops in the island, Major Peirson, decided to ignore the order to surrender. While Mulcaster sent the French envoys fleeing with cannon fire, Peirson's force, joined by men of the Jersey Militia, mustered on Westmount before advancing on the French who had fortified St Helier's market place, today the Royal Square. In the sharp battle that followed, the French were defeated, although 24-year-old Peirson was tragically killed leading his men into the square. De Rullecourt, wounded by musket fire in the battle, died the next day. At La Rocque, a force of regular British soldiers and the Jersey Militia also defeated the small French force left by De Rullecourt to defend his landing place.

Napoleonic Wars

The Battle of Jersey served to redouble military efforts in Jersey. The French Revolution, which occurred only a few years later, and subsequent rise of Napoleon Bonaparte, started a more or less continuous 25 year war between Britain and France, with Jersey a frontline outpost throughout. The island served as a base for naval raiding forces led by British Admiral Philip d'Auvergne that disrupted French coastal shipping and as headquarters for his spy and sabotage network of French émigrés intent on bringing down Napoleon. Although French forces massed opposite the island on occasions, no serious attempt was made to invade, perhaps because of the defences, which grew greatly in strength under the command of the island's latest lieutenant-governor, General Sir George Don.

Don took on the work started by General Conway with great vigour. He added three more round towers, those at Portelet, Noirmont and Icho, built or renovated more than fifty coastal batteries, and constructed barracks at places such as Grève de Lecq, Bonne Nuit and Rozel. One of his most important legacies that remains to this day is a network of military roads leading from St Helier to key strategic points on the island's coast to allow the swift movement of troops and guns. But General Don's most important effort, and his other major legacy, was a new principal fortress for the island, this time on a hill above St Helier.

The Battle of Jersey had underlined Elizabeth Castle's growing obsolescence. While it had not fallen, it was unable to prevent a French landing, or stop them capturing St Helier. General Don determined the island needed a more modern fortress, to sit at the heart of his defensive network. With the growing importance of the island's capital, the logical place to build it was on the heights called Mont de la Ville that towered over St Helier and so the foundation stone for Fort Regent, named after the then Prince Regent, was laid in 1806 with work completed in 1814. Within a year, however, there was peace in Europe as Napoleon fell from power. While the new state-of-the-art fortress would never be tested in battle, therefore, its mere presence must have made any would-be invader think twice about attacking Jersey.

The Victorian era

In the years immediately following the Battle of Waterloo, many of Jersey's fortifications were allowed to fall into disrepair or disappeared along with the perceived threat from France. The flawed nature of this policy became obvious as tensions between Britain and France increased once more in the 1830s, and Jersey found itself in a potential frontline situation once more. There was a renewed fortification programme as a result, with five additional round towers constructed – this time true Martello tower designs – in St Ouen's Bay, at La Collette, and on the hill overlooking Mont Orgueil Castle.

Several small forts appeared on the north coast, and there were new cannon emplaced at Elizabeth Castle. Finally, there was local clamour for a deep-water harbour capable of sheltering the British fleet, with St Catherine's Breakwater being the half-completed result.

In the 1840s, arsenals to house the militia cannon and weapons were built in St Mary, St Peter, St Lawrence, St Martin, Grouville and St Helier, thus ending the long-established practice of keeping cannons in the parish churches. In 1877, the militia itself – by then renamed The Royal Militia of the Island of Jersey as an honour for the part its men played in the Battle of Jersey – was reorganised from five infantry regiments to three, while the Royal Jersey Artillery came into existence, equipped with four gun batteries. By that time, however, just whom the militia was defending the island against came into question, as improving relations ended centuries of enmity between Britain and France. Yet, within decades, the two would become allies against Europe's rising new power, and Jersey would find itself armed and defended once more.

The Great War

In the years preceding 1914, there was considerable debate over the future of Jersey's defence. Britain was modernising its army, ready to play a part in an increasingly likely European war, and changing its defence strategy, which would see that army fighting alongside rather than against the French. In this new world of détente, there were questions over the need to keep a British Army garrison in Jersey, and the value and purpose of the local part-time forces.

By the outbreak of the First World War, therefore, and at the insistence of Britain, the militia had been modernised and reorganised once more, into a single infantry regiment of three battalions, the 1st (West) Battalion, the 2nd (East) Battalion and the 3rd (South or Town) Battalion. There was also a single regiment of artillery with two field batteries and two garrison companies together with an engineer company and a medical company. On 29 July 1914, in view of the deteriorating situation in Europe that followed the shooting of Archduke Franz Ferdinand in Sarajevo, the entire militia was mobilised to defend the island, taking up station at strategic points and around the coast. Many of the old fortifications and installations were reused at this time, for defence, accommodation and as command posts. When the British army garrison departed for overseas service in August 1914, the militia became the island's sole defenders, although further British soldiers did arrive for training in the island.

With the direct threat to Jersey receding towards the end of 1914 as trench warfare prevailed in France and Belgium, there was considerable pressure to send some of the militia to the war. In March 1915, the Jersey Contingent of 230 volunteers departed to serve in the British Army, later joined by nearly a hundred others to form the Jersey Company of the Royal Irish Rifles. They weren't alone. During the first two years of the war, hundreds more volunteers left the island to join the British Army, while more than 2,000 French nationals living or working in Jersey in 1914 departed to serve in the French Army. Coming the other way in 1915, were more than fifteen hundred German prisoners of war, housed in the newly built Blanches Banques POW Camp in St Ouen's Bay.

By 1916, it was clear the British Army could no longer rely on volunteers to meet its military commitments and replace the huge losses being experienced. A Military Service Act brought conscription to Britain at the start of that year, and the expectation was that Jersey and the other crown dependencies would follow. After lengthy negotiations, a similar act came into force in February 1917, compelling Jerseymen to serve in the British armed forces for the first time. Concurrently, the militia was temporarily disbanded and the defence of the island placed in the hands of a newly formed Royal Jersey Garrison Battalion, made up mainly from men unfit for overseas service.

The final two years of the First World War were very challenging for Jersey. Replacing the huge number of battlefield casualties demanded more and more of the island's men, while more and more island families experienced the loss of loved ones. The military demand for men meant women played an increasingly leading role in society, not just at home where they became heads of households but on the work front too as they took over many jobs traditionally undertaken by men. The island also had to contend with the threat of food and fuel shortages, as German submarines menaced cross-

Channel shipping and Britain demanded supplies for its war effort. The end of the war, when it came in November 1918, was timely, with Jersey facing an uncertain future had the fighting continued into 1919.

While the First World War may not have reached Jersey's shores directly, it had a profound impact on its population, the legacy of which is seen today on the island's many war memorials, most of which date to this period. Of the more than seven thousand men from Jersey who served in the armies of Britain and France, a shocking sixteen hundred lost their lives during the conflict or immediately after.

The Second World War

In the years between the First and Second World Wars, the defences of Jersey diminished considerably. The island's sole remaining coastal artillery battery, located on South Hill, was removed in 1929, shortly before the last British Army garrison departed. The Jersey Militia, which reformed in 1921 as a single infantry battalion, became a voluntary force in 1929 and reduced to a single company of 250 men. Like the men of an earlier generation, however, they too turned out to defend the island on the outbreak of war in 1939. In June 1940, as the Germans arrived on the nearby French coast after defeating the Allies in the Battle of France, these men together with a few regular soldiers were all that remained to defend the island. Sensibly, the British War Office decided not to put up a fight, and ordered the demilitarisation of the Channel Islands. As the last servicemen left, the militia went with them, to serve eventually in the Hampshire Regiment. Shortly thereafter, after a shock bombing raid to gauge the island's defences, the Germans arrived at the start of July to begin almost five years of occupation.

At first, the occupying forces made little attempt to fortify the island, believing that victory over Britain would quickly follow their triumph in France. It was only when this didn't happen, and after Hitler turned his attention to a war against the Soviet Union, that orders were given to turn the Channel Islands into impregnable fortresses. Along the coast, a network of defensive points were created, mostly categorised as either 'Strongpoint', 'Resistance Nest' or 'Operational Position', depending upon the number and complexity of their fortifications. Anti-tank walls went up along vulnerable beaches, while numerous artillery and anti-aircraft batteries were established on the coast and inland, with many of the guns installed in concrete emplacements. Railways linked the fortifications with ports and quarries while tunnels were bored and blasted into the sides of some of Jersey's valleys to hold the huge quantities of supplies and munitions needed to sustain the garrison in the event of a siege. Foreign workers undertook much of this construction work, some brought to the island voluntarily while others arrived as forced or slave labourers to live and work in desperately harsh conditions. In three years, they transformed the island into one of the most strongly fortified parts of Hitler's Atlantic Wall, created to defend the coast of Western Europe against Allied invasion, which by 1944 was imminent.

When it came, the Allies landed in nearby Normandy and fought for two months to break out from their bridgehead. Although Jersey's garrison was placed on full alert, no attempt was made to attack the island and the Germans here could do little or nothing to influence the fighting that eventually reached the nearby French coast. In August 1944, St Malo fell to the advancing American forces, thus isolating the German garrison in Jersey, and the island's inhabitants. An effective state of siege then existed until the end of the war, with the Allies unwilling to attack the island and the Germans, with little means to hit back. The result was a growing threat of starvation for both islanders and the German garrison alike, although the plight of the former was helped by the arrival of Red Cross parcels from December 1945 onwards.

As the war in Europe moved towards a conclusion, excitement among islanders rose. On 9 May 1945, British forces arrived to take the surrender of the German occupying forces, which has been celebrated as the island's Liberation Day ever since. Within days, most of the Germans were on ships bound for POW camps in Britain, while the huge task commenced of clearing their weapons of war and returning the island to normal.

The years since

After the Second World War, there was no question of Britain re-establishing a military presence in Jersey or a continuation of the militia, which formerly disbanded in 1946, although it was later resurrected in the guise of the Jersey Field Squadron, a Territorial Army unit representing the island's contribution to Britain's defence. There were some attempts immediately after the war to remove the now disarmed German fortifications and installations, but the effort needed meant that most were just sealed and landscaped over. As the Cold War commenced, however, the island's civil defence authorities took over a number of German bunkers for use as monitoring posts or headquarters in the event of a nuclear exchange. They remained as such until the end of the 20th century, when thankfully they were no longer deemed necessary. Other former German fortifications found new leases of life as museums or visitor attractions. While some have since closed, a number remain including the German Underground Hospital in St Peter's Valley, which today, as the Jersey War Tunnels, remains the most popular tourist destination in the island. Others have been restored by members of the Channel Islands Occupation Society to sit alongside earlier fortifications such as Mont Orgueil Castle and Elizabeth Castle as testaments to a most remarkable military history.

Opposite: The reclaimed gun mounting of Resistance Nest Richtfeurer near Liberation Station

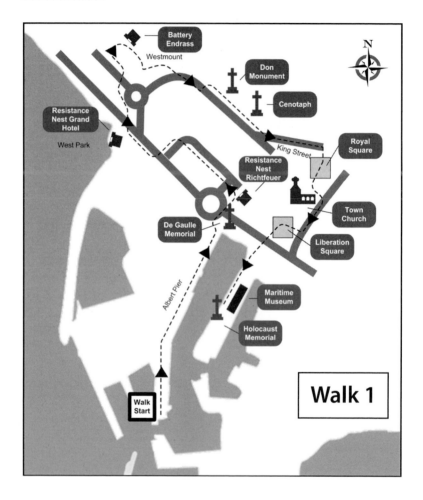

Walk 1: In Fateful Footsteps

The west of St Helier from its harbour to West Park and from Westmount to the Royal and Liberation Squares.

The emergence of St Helier as Jersey's principal settlement and port is a relatively recent event, although people have undoubtedly dwelt on the seashore there for thousands of years. It follows, therefore, that the military history of the island's capital only really began with the building of Elizabeth Castle at the start of the 17th century, although earlier defences may have existed. Since that time, however, St Helier has been the focus of considerable fortification development and military history related activity, as we find out on this packed walk around its western quarter.

Start:	End of the Albert Pier
Distance:	2.5 miles / 2 hours
Effort:	Moderate, although it is possible to bypass the one steep hill included
Getting There –	
By car:	Chargeable parking available outside the Elizabeth Harbour Terminal
By bus:	Walk from Liberation Station
Refreshments:	Numerous options en-route
Amenities:	Several public toilets en-route

Completed in 1853, the Albert Pier along with its sister Victoria Pier formed the outer arms of St Helier Harbour, growing rapidly at that time in both size and importance. Although they are not part of this walk, from the pier's end, we can see two of the island's major fortifications, both located nearby as a result of that growing importance, Elizabeth Castle on its islet outside the harbour's mouth, and Fort Regent dominating from the impressive heights of Mont de la Ville above. During the Occupation, the Germans also appreciated the importance of the harbour, constructing numerous installations to help defend and protect it, including **three large air-raid shelter bunkers** built on the Albert Pier and passed at the start of our walk. The first is immediately on the left as we walk away from the harbour mouth, conveniently painted white, which aids recognition and helps explain the method of bunker construction by highlighting the pattern of wooden shuttering into which concrete was poured.

A short distance away on the same side, is the first of several wall-mounted memorial tablets recalling important wartime events occurring here (although parked vehicles sadly conceal some at times). This first one commemorates the **arrival of SS *Vega*,** a Swedish Red Cross ship whose timely arrival in December 1944 saved islanders from looming starvation. What is not recalled is the less than straightforward process of getting it and its precious cargo to Jersey, with protracted negotiations between the Red Cross, the Germans and the British Government, with Prime Minister Winston Churchill reluctant to allow it in case food fell into enemy hands. For the increasingly desperate islanders, humanitarian common sense mercifully prevailed.

Continuing on, we pass another large German **air-raid shelter bunker,** this one retaining an **emplacement for a 2cm anti-aircraft gun** on top, before coming to the next memorial, which is dedicated to the memory of **islanders killed in a German air raid** just prior to the Jersey's occupation. Although Britain had ordered Jersey demilitarised in late 1940, it failed to notify the enemy in time to stop an air raid designed to gauge the island's defences. Sweeping across Mont de la Ville from the east, German warplanes bombed and machine gunned the harbour area, killing those commemorated here and wounding several others.

Continue along the pier, passing one of its two popular 'bacon roll' cafés before arriving at the next memorial, this one marking the **departure of the Jersey Militia** in June 1940. The Jersey Militia was a locally raised military force that had defended the island for more than seven hundred years, although by the Second World War it consisted of only a single company of around two hundred and fifty men. As the British Army pulled out in June 1940, the militiamen were faced with a dilemma: stay or go. Although not required to do so, virtually every man decided to leave and join the British Army, where many served with distinction in the years that followed.

After passing another large German **air-raid shelter bunker,** we reach three further memorials. One commemorates those who died in service during the Second World War, while the others recall another group of islanders who chose to leave in June 1940. With few means to defend Jersey from the approaching Germans, the British government offered to evacuate those civilians who wanted to leave, sending boats to St Helier Harbour to collect them. This caused considerable anxiety and tension, as people had only a matter of days to decide whether to leave or stay, with both choices fraught with uncertainty. In the end the majority decided to remain, but most of the 6,500 who made the choice to leave did so from here on the Albert Pier. Pause for a moment to imagine the scene as apprehensive people jostled to get on board clutching their few possessions, leaving behind friends and those family members who decided to stay, while on the walkway above some islanders jeered, seeing the evacuees as deserting in a time of crisis. It was definitely not one of the Jersey's proudest moments.

Continue on, passing the second café before reaching the base of the pier and its final and most recent memorial, which recalls **General De Gaulle's brief visit to Jersey** in June 1940. De Gaulle, who had just escaped by plane from a France about to surrender, was on his way to London where he soon established the Free French movement.

Turn left at the memorial, walking up the slope to turn right and cross the busy roundabout slip roads using the marked crossings. Going between the two office blocks, we pass Liberty Wharf on our right and find just after its entrance a **metal gun mounting** with an unusual history (see illustration page 23). During the Occupation, the Germans

built a small **bunker for a 4.7cm anti-tank gun** here to command the western approaches to town, this being the main road before land reclamation moved it further south. The bunker, part of a defensive position called *Resistance Nest Richtfeuer*, was demolished during a recent redevelopment but, under pressure from the Channel Islands Occupation Society, its steel gun mounting was incorporated into the new wall here, in virtually its original position.

With the gun mounting behind us, cross the road in front to walk in a westerly direction along the raised granite walkway running between the car park and former main road. At the end, use the marked crossings to reach the other side of the main road, turning right to pass Les Jardins de la Mer. The walk eventually brings us to West Park, where tickets are available for Elizabeth Castle, reached from here either on foot or by amphibious transports (popularly known as Ducks).

Before the Occupation, there was a small guardhouse associated with Elizabeth Castle here, whereas today the public toilets conceal a **bunker for a 4.7cm anti-tank gun**, part of the German's *Resistance Nest Grand Hotel*, which protected this end of St Aubin's Bay against invasion. Walking round the bunker and descending the steps to the beach, we find its steel gun mounting angled to sweep the beach in front and protected from fire by a huge concrete buttress clad in camouflaging granite. With a range of just under two miles, the gun, which was originally a Czechoslovakian weapon, would have been a formidable threat to anyone landing on this beach.

Although the Allies never attempted an invasion of Jersey during the Second World War, the sands between this bunker and Elizabeth Castle were the scene of a bloody battle more than five hundred years earlier. In 1406, a force of raiders under the command of a Castilian nobleman called Pero Niño landed on the islet where Elizabeth Castle stands today and threatened the island. Drawn up here to oppose him were Jersey's defenders, which included men of the early militia. Following a hard fought encounter, Niño managed to overcome the local forces, who fell back before fighting another battle that reportedly took place on or near Grouville Hill. Another defeat there and Jersey had little choice but to pay off Niño and his men.

Leaving the beach and bunker, cross the main road once more using the pedestrian crossings here, before walking up the gentle slope towards the impressive West Park Apartments set against the cliff face. If you prefer not to climb up to Westmount Hill towering above the apartments, turn right before reaching them and follow the road around People's Park to re-join the walk opposite the Shipwright Pub. For those happy to make the ascent, remain on the pavement across the road from the apartments, passing in front of them until the greenery of West Park Gardens appears on the slope opposite, with a small granite entrance that we go through after carefully crossing the road. Take the steps up through the gardens until reaching a level path that we follow past the half-round open area to take the steeply rising steps on our right. Climb them to the top, turn right and then walk until you reach the large concrete structure jutting out into the path.

We have reached the command and fire control post of Battery Endrass, a German artillery battery of four 10.5cm guns situated in bunkers where the houses behind now stand. Its purpose was to block access to St Helier Harbour, where we started our walk, and with a range of just over seven miles, Endrass was capable of firing directly at any ship that approached. Today, the guns are gone, although some of the battery's bunkers remain situated on private land.

Going round the bunker, continue along the path to the road where we turn right, noting the **plaque commemorating Westmount's part in the Battle of Jersey.** As we reach the hairpin bend, stop to consider St Helier below, and the events of that landmark day in 1781.

When **Major Peirson assembled his troops** here prior to advancing into St Helier, he would have had a very different outlook. The town in those days was just a cluster of buildings centred on the Royal Square and Town Church, the steeple of which is visible almost directly below the Signal Station on Fort Regent. The fort itself did not exist – work on it started 25 years later in 1806. Between the town and here was open ground, filled with fields, orchards and

Major Peirson, the 24-year-old commander who won victory over the French invaders in 1781

sand dunes, although a building used as soldier's barracks existed on the site of today's General Hospital. Nevertheless, it may be possible to imagine the sense of excitement and trepidation among the men standing here who were both regular British soldiers and Jersey militiamen. With their senior officers out of the island, in command was the 24-year-old major, while waiting in the town below was an enemy force of unknown strength, but ready to defend itself. Peirson's men were about to find out how ready. The next part of our walk follows – roughly at least – in their footsteps as they advanced on the Royal Square for a confrontation with De Rullecourt's invaders.

Follow the steps down from Westmount to cross People's Park and arrive at the far corner, opposite the Shipwright Pub. Cross the road here, turn left and then quickly right to walk through the Parade passing the General Hospital. In the gardens on the left is an impressive statue flanked by cannon that we will cross the road to inspect.

This is the **Don Monument**, erected in 1885 to commemorate General Sir George Don, the island's lieutenant-governor between 1806 and 1814, during the height of the Napoleonic Wars. Don did much to improve Jersey's defences at the time, including the building of military roads, round towers, barracks and, most significantly, Fort Regent on the heights above town. He also helped establish this large area of open land as a parade ground for soldiers, so it appropriate to find his statue here.

Walking away from the monument towards town again, after crossing a road we reach **the Cenotaph**, Jersey's principal memorial to its dead of the two world wars. The dreadful fighting of the First World War had an enormous impact on the island, with more than 1,600 Jerseymen losing their lives. Soon after its end in 1918, Jersey began erecting memorials to honour their sacrifice, including this one built in 1920. In the small sarcophagus on top rests two 'Rolls of Honour', one with the names of those who died in the First World War and one for those of the Second.

Continue on this side of the road, passing **St Helier's Town Hall** on the opposite side, used between 1940 and 1945 by the occupying German forces. Just inside the main doors is a **memorial naming islanders killed during the Second World War** while serving in the armed forces. Note that the Town Hall was also where locals wanting to leave in June 1940 queued in large numbers to register for evacuation prior to the Occupation, while set in the pavement outside are a number of **poignant quotations** from individuals who lived through that period.

After a short distance, we reach Charing Cross where the road splits into King Street and Broad Street and are faced with the same choice as Major Peirson in 1781. At the time of the Battle of Jersey, Charing Cross marked roughly the edge of town, and here Peirson spilt his main force, with one column advancing up Broad Street while the other, led by the Major, marched up King Street, then a smaller back road called Rue de Derrière. Taking King Street, we follow it for about three hundred metres until reaching a cut on the right hand side, today called **Peirson Place**, which leads into the Royal Square, then the town's market place. On the left is a pub bearing

Peirson's name and picture, with its wall above eye-level having a number of small circular marks said to be caused by musket fire from that fateful day. The outnumbered French forces were in the Royal Square ahead, defending each entrance with cannon and small arms. Undeterred, Peirson advanced into the square here, only to be hit and killed by musket fire. Despite the loss, his men rallied, and took the square thus winning the Battle of Jersey and ensuring the island remained British.

Entering the square, cross to the golden statue of King George II on his plinth and contemplate the setting. The Royal Square is bounded on one side by the imposing States Building where Jersey's government meets. It was from the balcony near its main entrance that Islanders heard on 8 May 1945 that the war had ended and they were to be liberated. Standing there that day was the wartime Bailiff, Alexander Coutanche, and his bust is found underneath the balcony along with a memorial tablet. Imagine his moment of relief and triumph that day having come through five years of occupation, and the joyous cheers of the gathered crowd in the square.

Thirty years earlier, there was another cheering crowd here on the early morning of 2 March 1915 when volunteers from the Jersey Militia paraded on this spot prior to their departure for Ireland and service with the Royal Irish Rifles during the First World War. Of 326 who joined, eighty, or one in four, died while serving. On that day, the men of the Jersey Contingent, as they were known, marched off the square towards the Town Church, situated across the road from the States Building, on their way to the harbour, and our walk follows them. Before departing, however, note the word *Vega* set into the paving stones in front of statue, recalling the arrival of the Red Cross ship during the last winter of the Occupation.

Leaving the Royal Square, walk towards the Town Church, parts of which have stood on this site since the 10th or 11th centuries. An optional visit inside will find Major Peirson's grave in front of the altar, while that of the French commander, Baron De Rullecourt is somewhere in the churchyard. A small stone bearing his name exists, but the actual site of burial is today lost. Also in the church are flags and colours of the Jersey Militia, laid up here after it disbanded in

1946. Our walk turns left, noting in the churchyard, opposite the States Buildings, the gravestone of Richard Henly, who was surgeon of Russian troops stationed in the island at the time of the Napoleonic Wars. The date stated is 1815, although the Russians were actually here between 1798 and 1799 as a contribution to the coalition then existing between England and Russia against the French.

Our walk then turns right to follow the road down from Hill Street into Mulcaster Street, named in honour of Captain Mulcaster who held Elizabeth Castle against the French invaders at the time of the Battle of Jersey. Walk straight ahead, crossing the roads using the pedestrian crossings, until you reach **Liberation Square**. Stop in front of the statue.

Philip Jackson's initially controversial memorial to Jersey's Liberation

This square, created in its current form in 1995 to mark the 50th anniversary of Jersey's liberation, is the focal point for the annual celebrations that continue to mark that momentous day in the island's history. The area is replete with reminders and memorials from the Second World War. The bronze statue itself, set on a plinth and surrounded by twelve water jets symbolising Jersey's twelve parishes, is the work of renowned sculptor Philip Jackson. Although today it is an accepted element of the square, its commissioning back in the early 1990s was a stormy and controversial one. The original design proposed to mark 50 years of peace rather than 50 years since liberation, and featured released doves rather than the waving flag.

Amid a storm of claims that it failed to capture the spirit of that 1945 day, the commissioning committee gave way and asked for the revised design we see today. Even then it didn't please everyone, including those who thought the ensemble were waving washing rather than raising a flag, but in the years since it has grown in acclaim.

Directly behind the statue is the for mer railway terminus for the Jersey Western Railway, and from the rear of which over one thousand people were deported in 1942 to internment camps in Germany, a move ordered by Hitler in response to the internment of German civilians in Iran. A plaque commemorating this event can be found on the right-hand side of the building. To the right of the statue, across the road, is the imposing façade of the Pomme d'Or Hotel. During the Occupation, the Germans had requisitioned the building to serve as their naval headquarters, complete with a huge air-raid shelter bunker built on the left-hand corner, demolished in the 1960s with its place taken today by the café we can see. It was on the balcony of this hotel that British forces after landing on 9 May 1945 went to unfurl a Union flag in front of thousands gathered in this place to mark the end of the Occupation.

Leave Liberation Square and cross over the road to reach the harbour once again. The pier ahead is the New North Quay, from where the Jersey Contingent departed in 1915. A walk along it brings us to Jersey's Holocaust Memorial, commemorating the twenty-two islanders who died in German camps and prisons. It stands outside the Maritime Museum, part of which is dedicated to displaying the

Occupation Tapestry. Unveiled in 1995 on the 50th anniversary of liberation, it consists of twelve hand-woven panels depicting scenes from the five years of occupation. In 2016, a thirteenth commissioned to mark the 70th anniversary of Liberation was added. A visit is highly recommended, before returning to Albert Pier and the end of our walk.

The Jersey Contingent departs St Helier Harbour's New North Quay in March 1915

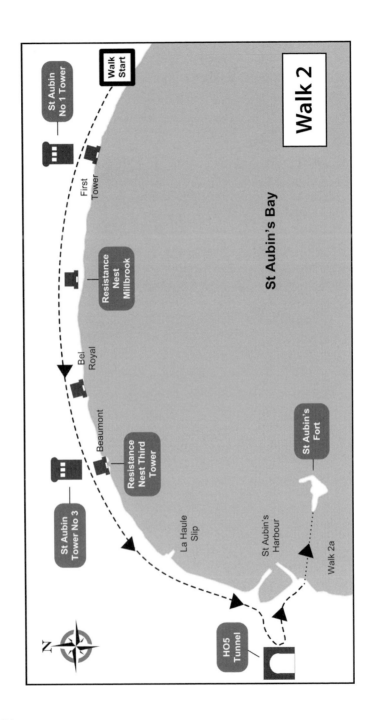

Walk 2

St Aubin's Bay

St Aubin No 1 Tower

Walk Start

First Tower

Resistance Nest Millbrook

Bel Royal

Beaumont

Resistance Nest Third Tower

St Aubin Tower No 3

La Haule Slip

St Aubin's Fort

St Aubin's Harbour

Walk 2a

HO5 Tunnel

N

Conway-style round tower at First Tower

Walk 2: Swept Sands

Around St Aubin's Bay from First Tower to St Aubin's Village and Harbour, with optional visit to St Aubin's Fort

The wide sandy expanse of St Aubin's Bay curves between the island's present day capital and the village of St Aubin, which was once Jersey's chief port and centre for commerce. The presence of these two important locations, together with the bay's obvious attraction for any seaborne invader, has resulted in significant fortifications here since the late 16th century, including Elizabeth Castle and St Aubin's Fort as offshore strongpoints. This long but easy walk takes in the many interesting fortifications located along the shoreline, before an optional visit across the sands to St Aubin's Fort.

Start:	First Tower
Distance:	3.5 miles / 3 hours
Effort:	Easy, though suitable beach footwear recommended to visit St Aubin's Fort
Getting there –	
By car:	Chargeable parking available along Victoria Avenue
By bus:	Walk from Liberation Station
Refreshments:	Several beach cafés and restaurants along the bay, with plenty more around St Aubin's Harbour.
Amenities:	Several public toilets en-route

Walk along the seafront until reaching First Tower where we start our walk. The wide walkway found here is the former route of the **Jersey Western Railway**, which ran from St Helier to St Aubin and then on to Corbière on the island's extreme south-west point. During the Occupation, the Germans used the same route for a railway of their own, built to move materials between construction sites and munitions to fortifications. Today the rails of both are long gone, but beware of straying onto the tracks of the cycle path and into the way of fast moving cyclists who can approach from behind without warning.

At First Tower, cyclists have to go round a large grass mound concealing a German **bunker for a 4.7cm anti-tank gun** angled to fire along the beach as part of **Resistance Nest First Tower**. There are four of a very similar design found along the bay, all constructed on top of slipways that once led down to the beach – an expedient way of blocking them to any potential invaders. In certain conditions, the sands shift to reveal the ghostly remains of the missing slipways while the granite blocks recovered from them were used to camouflage some of the bunkers including this one. Today, although now empty of its gun, the aperture through which it once fired still sweeps the sands to remind us of the deadly killing field that would have existed during the war.

Across the road from the bunker stands an earlier fortification also placed here to sweep these sands with deadly fire. Despite its name of First Tower, the **St Aubin No. 1 Tower**, was not the first built in Jersey as is sometimes believed, but rather the first of three towers situated in St Aubin's Bay. All three are Conway-style round towers, positioned to command the beach and defend the entrances to valleys leading inland from the foreshore. When this one was constructed in the late 18th century, it would have stood closer to the shoreline, among the dunes that lined the bay, and fired at any invaders using a 24-pounder cannon mounted on top.

Leaving First Tower continue along the bay passing the Old Station Café at Millbrook on the right – a reminder of the former railway heritage – shortly before reaching another German **bunker for a 4.7cm anti-tank gun**, very similar in design to that visited at First Tower. In contrast, however, this one is far from empty and derelict having been restored by the Channel Islands Occupation

Society. Originally part of the German *Resistance Nest Millbrook*, which was responsible for defending this part of the bay, it was sealed soon after the war. When reopened in 1985, despite missing its gun and a steel observation cupola on top, the bunker was in almost perfect condition. With an identical gun recovered from France, today the bunker opens to the public on occasions, with a visit highly recommended.

Continuing from Millbrook, we arrive at Bel Royal with a third **bunker for a 4.7cm anti-tank gun** on the far side of the slip, and a domed concrete structure on the other, both of which were part of the Germans' **Resistance Nest Bel Royal**. This was a **heavy machine gun bunker** once topped with a huge steel turret and armed with two machine guns to pour fire onto the beach below. The turret fell victim to scrap men in 1953, who removed it and capped the bunker with the concrete plug visible today. While the slip here was not removed, a concrete passageway that once linked the two bunkers blocked it.

Another lost element to Bel Royal's fortifications is **St Aubin No. 2 Tower**, the second Conway-style round tower in St Aubin's Bay. It stood roughly where the hamburger stand is now, again armed with a cannon on top during the Napoleonic Wars. When building their defences, however, the Germans decided it blocked all round fire from the machine gun bunker and demolished the unfortunate tower in January 1943.

Note that the anti-tank gun bunker, which ironically has the date '1943' inscribed above the gun embrasure, extends to a small **one-man bunker** above the beach known as a 'tobruk stand'. These extremely common fortifications were either open, or capped with a tank turret armed with a machine gun or anti-tank gun. It is located at the start a concrete anti-tank wall, designated PzM7 (*PzM standing for Panzermauern or anti-tank wall*), and built by a mix of skilled and slave labour. Construction was carried out in separate sections locked together using a 'tongue and groove' system, examples of which are visible as we walk along. The different heights and styles on this wall appear to have come about due to shortages in cement. Some way along, note also a fake bunker constructed to confuse any potential invader complete with apparent gun embrasure.

Continuing on we reach Beaumont, and a third Conway-style

round tower, called Beaumont Tower, or **St Aubin No. 3 Tower,**
constructed in the 1780s like the others in St Aubin's Bay. The
Germans placed a machine gun on its top during the Occupation,
and built a number of fortifications around to form *Resistance Nest
Third Tower.* Here we also find a **bunker for a 10.5cm gun,** which in
contrast to the others passed on our walk fired out to sea rather than
along the beach. Today it forms part of the popular Gunsite Café,
while on either side are **one man bunkers** and next to the slip is a
small **bunker for a tank turret** fitted with an anti-tank gun.

*The bunker
now used as
Beaumont's
Gunsite Café
during the
Occupation
(CIOS Collection)*

Leaving Beaumont, continue towards St Aubin passing a car park
on the right before reaching some public toilets. In this area, the
concrete anti-tank wall briefly gives way to granite before rearing
up in a **final short span of concrete** once again. The explanation for
this is that the Germans never fully finished this section but did lay
the foundations. Years later, the granite stretch of wall here was built
on those foundations, competing the job of the occupying forces and
creating something of a design conundrum for the casual observer.
Continuing, we pass La Haule Slip complete with a small **bunker
for a tank turret** once armed with a 3.7cm anti-tank gun, before
reaching St Aubin.

Prior to the emergence of St Helier as the main port of Jersey
during the 17th century, St Aubin was the centre for much of the
island's shipping and commerce, with many fine buildings and place
names to remind us of that time. Our walk takes us into St Aubin

through the cut between the public toilets and Parish Hall, or Salle Parioissiale, itself once the railway station of St Aubin. From here the railway line went north, and we follow its former route, crossing the road to walk along the pavement in front of the building today housing Natwest Bank. After twenty metres, while the main road continues to our right, ahead a cut between two buildings leads to the start of the Corbière Walk.

Just as the walk starts, there is an enormous **concrete wall complete with machine gun loophole** on the left, behind which lies the entrance to a tunnel. The tunnel was originally constructed in the 19th century to take the railway through the protruding hillside here. The Germans widened it during the Occupation, and bored a new tunnel, designated HO5 (*HO standing for Hohlgangsanlagen, or cave passage installation*), into its left hand wall from which side chambers branched off for the storage of fuel and ammunition.

Leaving the tunnel, we retrace our steps back to the harbour side, turning right to walk along the Bulwarks until reaching the start of the harbour's southern arm. In this area, the Germans created *Resistance Nest Hafen Aubin*, the only remaining part of which is a **bunker for a 4.7cm anti-tank gun and a tank turret** armed with a machine gun towards the end of the pier.

Here our walk ends, leaving the choice of stopping for refresh-ments before returning to St Helier on foot or by bus from the Parish Hall or in the summer by Le Petit Train which drives between St Helier and St Aubin throughout the day. If the tide is down (make doubly sure it is not coming up), you may like to take a stroll out to St Aubin's Fort.

Mounting for a 4.7cm anti-tank gun high up in the outside wall of St Aubin's Harbour

Walk 2a: St Aubin's Fort

This optional walk starts outside the Royal Channel Islands Yacht Club located on the end of St Aubin's Bulwarks, at the top of the slip down to the beach here and the causeway leading out to St Aubin's Fort.

The first fortification constructed on the islet here was a tower and cannon battery believed to have been built between 1542 and 1545 to defend the harbour of St Aubin, then the island's principal port. Rebuilt and expanded over the years that followed, by the time of the English Civil War it mounted five cannon that played a part in the local fighting associated with this period. But as St Helier grew in importance in the years that followed, and St Aubin diminished, so too did the need for a fort. There was something of a renaissance, however, with the arrival of the Germans in 1940 and their work to re-arm the fort once more.

St Aubin's Fort is surrounded at high tide, so any visit must coincide with low water, ideally as it ebbs giving us plenty of time to get there and back. Go onto the beach and across the causeway, noting the **4.7cm anti-tank gun steel mounting** in the harbour wall high up to our left. After going up the slip to reach the fort's walls, one of the first things to be noted behind the cluster of small boats is a **German personnel shelter bunker** built for the garrison who would have used the small passage cut through the wall to access the fort's interior. Continue towards the large **bunker for a 10.5cm gun**, which would have been used in conjunction with another gun of the same type at Elizabeth Castle opposite to block access to the bay.

To the side of the bunker is the fort's entrance gateway, with the date 1742 carved into its keystone, denoting a time when many of the modifications present today were built. The interior of the fort is private, being used by Jersey's Youth Service as an outdoor centre, so we should only enter if we have permission to do so. Inside are gun platforms and associated magazines as well as a small German **bunker for a tank turret** that until fairly recently still mounted its turret.

Returning to the harbourside, we find another bunker for a

tank turret at the end of the short pier and a third through a small doorway at the base of the pier that leads to a former **18th century gun position and magazine.**

St Aubin's Fort, with German bunker for a 10.5cm gun in the foreground

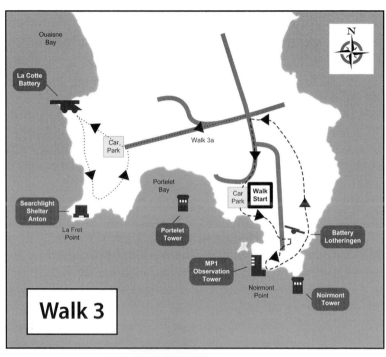

Walk 3

Ouaisne Bay

La Cotte Battery

Car Park

Walk 3a

Searchlight Shelter Anton

La Fret Point

Portelet Bay

Portelet Tower

Car Park

Walk Start

Battery Lotheringen

MP1 Observation Tower

Noirmont Point

Noirmont Tower

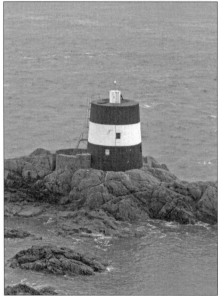

Noirmont Tower, one of three built by General Don during the Napoleonic Wars

Walk 3: Anchored Battleship

A ramble from Portelet through the fortifications of Noirmont Point with an optional visit to Portelet Common and La Fret Point.

At Noirmont Point on Jersey's south-west coast the land meets the sea in a particularly dramatic fashion. The rocky headland rearing up from the waves here dominates the route taken by many ships travelling to and from St Aubin's Bay, making it a choice location for fortifications intended to protect or disrupt that passage. During the Occupation, the Germans certainly recognised this and placed great emphasis on fortifying the Noirmont headland and its flanking cliffs. On this walk, we visit the well-preserved results of those efforts and others, while enjoying some of Jersey's most spectacular coastal views.

Start:	Portelet Car Park
Length:	2 miles / 1.5 hours (3.5 mile / 2.5 hours if Portelet Common and La Fret Point are visited)
Difficulty:	Easy
Getting there –	
By car:	Free parking in Portelet Car Park
By bus:	Route 12a from Liberation Station, alighting at Portelet Car Park
Refreshments:	The Old Portelet Inn, where our walk starts and ends
Amenities:	Aside from those located in the Old Portelet Inn, there are no public toilets en-route

From Portelet Car Park, take the footpath that starts in its right-hand corner. There are soon fine views over Portelet Bay, with its picturesque central islet complete with small round tower.

Portelet Tower was one of three built during the Napoleonic Wars on the orders of General Don, then the island's lieutenant-governor. They were different in design to the more numerous Conway-style round towers constructed earlier by one of his predecessors, being typically stouter and lacking the protruding defences, or machiolations, around the top. This one, constructed in 1808, is one of the smallest with only a single storey. At times, the tower is wrongly called 'Janvrin's Tomb', which refers to a sea captain called Philippe Janvrin who was buried on the islet after dying of plague while at sea – long before this tower was built.

Follow the path, which leaving Portelet skirts the edge of Noirmont Point headland. After a short distance, the first German construction comes into view ahead on the right, a large and rather rudimentary **personnel shelter bunker** standing out from the undergrowth. Passing it by, we continue walking until reaching another concrete structure on the left-hand side of the path, this time a large **concrete gun platform**. Climb carefully up the earth bank to enter the platform through its broken side, then pause to consider what lies in front of us.

The Germans built **Battery Lothringen** at Noirmont Point to accommodate four 15cm heavy naval guns, whose primary role was to fire on ships approaching or passing the island. Each gun stood on a raised open emplacement, such as this one which was called **Gun Position No. 4**, while nearby were one or two underground ammunition bunkers and a personnel shelter for the gun crew. The ones associated with this platform are lost under the undergrowth, but we see examples later on the walk. A massive command bunker located on the tip of the headland controlled the firing of the four guns, while anti-aircraft guns, smaller artillery guns, flamethrowers, machine guns and barbed wire protected the whole battery. From this vantage point, many of the emplacements and shelters for all these weapons and their crews are visible, with many visited on our walk.

After coming back down from the platform, follow the footpath again until reaching the tarmac road that cuts through the headland.

Cross over to arrive at **Gun Position No. 1** complete with an original gun barrel restored once more to the emplacement. After the Occupation, the British Army removed the guns here at Noirmont and dumped them over cliffs at Les Landes on the island's north-west coast, together with all the other heavy guns in the island. But after languishing for years at the bottom of the cliffs, the Channel Islands Occupation Society (CIOS) recovered a number of gun barrels for display, including this one now installed on a replica mounting. To complete the picture, the CIOS cleared this gun position's complex of associated bunkers and ramps, revealing the remarkable extent and complexity of the construction work undertaken here.

After inspecting this group of fortifications, go back to the road and turn left to walk past a **water storage bunker** and a restored **anti-aircraft emplacement** on the left. On the opposite side, there is another cleared ammunition bunker and the raised emplacement for **Gun Position No. 3** to inspect before arriving at the public car park at the end of the road. Bear right here to pass another opened and partially restored **personnel shelter bunker** to reach the walkway taking us on top of the huge concrete tower situated here on the end of the headland.

This remarkable **naval observation tower** was designated MP1 (*MP standing for Marinepeilstände und Meßstellen or Naval Coastal Artillery Direction and Range-finding Position*) by the Germans who built it in 1942. One of three completed in the island out of nine planned, its role was to observe the marine approaches, directing artillery fire not just from the guns here at Noirmont but from any of the island's heavy batteries, against potentially multiple enemy targets. Today under the care of the CIOS, who open it to the public from time to time, it also has an **original mounting for a 2cm anti-aircraft gun** in the emplacement on top.

From the top of MP1, the strategic importance of Noirmont Point is understandable. It commands the approaches to St Helier Harbour, in particular those coming along the south-west coast of Jersey from Guernsey and the UK. During the Napoleonic Wars, this importance led to General Don building **Noirmont Tower**, or Tour de Vinde as it was called, on rocks at the bottom of the cliffs here between 1810 and

1814. Today painted in bright colours as a navigation aid, when built it mounted a cannon on top and one at the base.

Continuing our walk, leave MP1 and turn right towards the steel domes and apparatus visible a short distance away. These mark the location of the Battery Lothringen's two-storey **command and fire control bunker,** constructed in a pit blasted out of the headland (note the extracted rocks cascading away down the cliff) to house the men and equipment needed to aim and fire the four heavy guns. For pinpointing targets far out at sea, the two smaller domes once contained powerful periscopes while the larger housed a range finder in its two metal arms. A little way beyond the domes is the command bunker's entrance, nearby which are a number of anti-tank obstacles recovered from around the island and subsequently placed here. Once again, the CIOS have restored this installation to an extremely high standard over many years and regularly open it to the public.

The periscopes and range finder of Battery Lothringen's command and control bunker on the headland at Noirmont

Mounted beside the bunker's entrance is a **small memorial** commemorating the death of two **RAF pilots** shot down and killed while attacking German shipping off Noirmont Point in 1942. On that day, a number of Whirlwinds from 263 Squadron, which

The Westland Whirlwind was a rare British fighter-bomber during the Second World War, but two were lost off Noirmont Point in 1942

had the specific role of striking enemy coastal shipping and installations, attacked a German convoy of four ships making its way towards St Helier Harbour. They managed to sink one vessel and damage another, although the cost was two planes lost to anti-aircraft fire, with the remains of Squadron Leader Woodward and Warrant Officer Don McPhail never found. Spare a thought for them and the German naval dead of the battle as you look out from here.

From the command bunker entrance, walk to the right across the car park towards the final raised gun emplacement, noting on the left a memorial stone commemorating the government of Jersey's acquisition of this whole headland after the Occupation as a memorial to those islanders who lost their lives during the Second World War. Lying behind the memorial stone is another impressive complex of ammunition bunkers and access ramps associated with the gun emplacement that we are visiting next.

Climb up the ramp to **Gun Position No. 2,** which like the others would have mounted a 15cm naval gun, a weapon capable of firing at targets as far as ten miles away. The barrel currently in the emplacement is not one originally located at Noirmont, however, although it is from another type of 15cm gun. In 1944, after the nearby French coast fell to the Allies, the Germans decided to move eight modern heavy guns from Guernsey to Jersey in order to reinforce this island's now exposed eastern coastline. Like all the others, these were dumped over the cliffs at the end of the war, although this one never made it to the bottom, ending up tantalisingly visible half way down. It was the first gun recovered, and with no other obvious location to install it came here to Noirmont Point in 1976.

Heavy 15cm naval gun recovered from the bottom of the cliffs and returned to its former home at Noirmont Point

After leaving the emplacement, turn right and follow the winding cliff path that starts here and leads past a **personnel shelter bunker** before reaching another memorial, itself situated on the foundations of a former German mess hut.

This is a **memorial to American sailors killed in action off Noirmont Point** in August 1944 in a night time battle between US Navy PT (Patrol Torpedo) boats and a German convoy ironically bringing the heavy guns from Guernsey to Jersey. PT boats were developed before the Second World War as small high-speed vessels armed with torpedoes for

American PT Boats of the type engaged in battle off Noirmont on August 1944

use against enemy shipping. They served in both the Pacific and Atlantic Oceans, proving remarkably effective against targets often much larger than themselves. On the night of 9–10 August 1944, a number of them left Allied-held Cherbourg to intercept the German convoy and a running battle ensued as the heavily armed German vessels fought back. A little way off Noirmont Point, the badly damaged **PT509** rammed a German minesweeper and exploded.

Only one of its 15-man crew survived the battle, while two other US sailors died on another PT boat. The Germans suffered four dead and one man missing as well as many wounded in this bitter little encounter.

Leaving the memorial, follow the path as it winds around the headland, noting further bunkers and installations on both sides and pausing now and then to take in the stunning vista of St Aubin's Bay. Continue along the path, which skirts a chain-link fence denoting private property on the eastern side of the headland, for about 500 metres, passing through the woods until reaching the main road leading to Portelet and Noirmont Point. If returning to the starting point at this time, turn left and remain on this road back to Portelet Car Park. To visit the fortifications of Portelet Common, however, take the road opposite leading away from the crossroads here and walk about 100 metres to a fork in the road and a sign indicating the left-hand way leads to Portelet Common.

Walk 3a: Portelet Common and Le Fret Point

After a short walk, we pass the site of the former Portelet Hotel, used by members of the German Air Force during the early days of the Occupation, before they and their planes moved to other fronts in 1941. After a further walk, we arrive at a small car park and take the footpath on the right-hand side that leads more or less straight ahead. In due course, we reach the cliff edge and surely one of the finest coastal views in Jersey. To the right a small white building is discernible together with a narrow footpath leading towards it. Follow this until we reach a granite platform overlooking the sea.

La Cotte Battery dates back to 1759 when a gun platform and a magazine was built on this lofty vantage point to protect against enemy landings in the bay below. At the time of the Napoleonic Wars some fifty years later, it mounted two 18-pounder cannon capable of firing round shot up to a range of nearly one mile. Envy the gunners stationed here on a beautiful day, but pity those trying to shelter in a storm with the wind howling and waves crashing on the rocks far below.

After retracing our steps from the battery, turn right onto a footpath that follows the headland towards a granite wall in the distance. Follow the path alongside that wall until a gate is reached through which we pass, noting that some areas of the headland in front are private property and should be respected as such. Take the right-hand path, to continue along the edge of the headland until on the left (it may be obscured by vegetation) we encounter the first German fortification, this one a **personnel shelter bunker** with two entrances and two observation stands. It and several others formed *Resistance Nest Le Fret*, the German defensive position here. Returning to the path, a short distance further on are several concrete installations on the right including a large **garage bunker** that still contains the rusting remains of machinery once probably used to winch supplies down to other bunkers below. Continue along the path and the first of these comes into sight, a **searchlight shelter** bunker for a 60cm searchlight used to illuminate the bay below at night. A scramble down is challenging but does allow us to inspect the bunker and the ramp onto which the searchlight would have emerged. Below this bunker, and much harder to reach, is a **bunker for a 10.5cm gun** angled to fire into St Brelade's Bay. Unlike most of its contemporaries, the gun was not removed from this bunker after the war, remaining in place for those nimble enough to find a way down until recovered in recent years and shipped to Guernsey where is sits today in a restored bunker at Fort Hommet on that island's west coast.

Local children examine searchlight Anton after the Occupation in its headland bunker at Le Fret Point (CIOS Collection)

There is one more German bunker to visit here on the headland, and one situated in a most dramatic location. Carefully follow the path further until reaching a **searchlight shelter bunker** that would have protected Anton, a 150cm searchlight associated with Battery Lothringen on Noirmont Point. The rails on which Anton would have moved in and out of its shelter are still present on the concrete platform overlooking the cliff edge and from where its light would have been used to illuminate targets far out to sea.

Leaving Anton, we retrace our steps back to the gate in the granite wall. Take the right-hand path through the trees until the car park is reached and the road back past the former Portelet Hotel. From there it is back to the main road, a right turn and walk back to Portelet Car Park and our starting point.

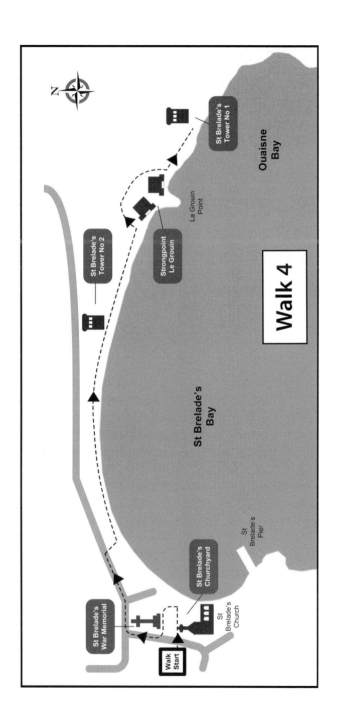

Walk 4: Deceptively Calm

From St Brelade's Churchyard to Le Grouin Point and over for a visit to the quiet of Ouaisné Common.

There is no denying that the beautiful bays of St Brelade and Ouaisné are among the island's finest, and yet the contrast between the two, separated only by the gnarled promontory of Le Grouin Point, could hardly be more marked. Developed or natural, however, the gently sloping beaches and sheltered approaches make both an obvious choice for any invader, a threat that led to the fortification of both through the centuries. On this short and very pleasant walk, we discover the remains of these fortifications among the rich military history of this deceptively calm part of Jersey.

Start:	St Brelade's Churchyard
Length:	One and half miles / one and a half hours
Difficulty:	Easy
Getting there –	
By car:	Chargeable parking in St Brelade's Bay
By bus:	Route 12 from Liberation Station, alighting at St Brelade's Church
Refreshments:	A wide choice of restaurants, bars and cafés along St Brelade's Bay
Amenities:	Public toilets in St Brelade's and Ouaisné Bays

Our walk begins at the covered gateway in front of the church's main entrance, and starts with a visit to the interior of St Brelade's Church, which can trace its origins back to the 5th or 6th centuries. There are a number of interesting memorials with a military connection inside, including one to Ernest (Victor) Briard, who was **the first Jerseyman killed in the First World War**. Ernest died during the fighting at Mons in August 1914, although in the confusion of war his family were unable to confirm his death until 1916, holding out hope that he was actually a prisoner-of-war. Sadly, the Briard family also had to endure the death of his younger brother John four years later, killed while fighting on India's Northwest Frontier.

Left: St Brelade's War Memorial with its 59 names from the two World Wars and the Troubles in Northern Ireland

Right: Captain Ernest (Victor) Briard, the first Jerseymen killed in the First World War and whose memorial is found today inside St Brelade's Church

Leave the church and follow the path that leads around it and past the 11th century Fisherman's Chapel, used from the 16th until mid-18th centuries to **house the parish cannon of the Jersey Militia**. Ahead the magnificent panorama of St Brelade's and Ouaisné Bays comes into view. Once you have reached the wall overlooking the beach, stop for a moment to consider the setting.

From this vantage point, the bay's appeal to potential invaders is understandable, offering sheltered waters and gently sloping beaches.

During the Napoleonic Wars, this appeal led to no fewer than 18 cannons being placed around the bay in several locations, including three 12-pounder cannon mounted here in the **Churchyard Battery**. Together, they would have created a deadly crossfire to oppose anyone trying to land.

Follow the path alongside the wall before turning left to pass the large gate leading to the beach slipway. To its left we find a memorial recalling that this part of the churchyard was once the location of a large and not entirely welcome military cemetery.

During the First World War, St Brelade's churchyard was chosen to bury seven German prisoners-of-war who died at the **Blanche Banques First World War POW Camp** situated in St Ouen's Bay (see Walk 6). When the Germans arrived in 1940, the presence of these graves made this the natural location for all **German military burials during the Occupation**, so between 1940 and 1945 a further 207 men were buried here (the memorial on the wall states an incorrect number of 337 burials). The dead were victims of accidents, enemy action or illness, the latter particularly the case as the war progressed and older soldiers arrived to replace the younger men. Here they remained after the war, although the original grave markers complete with swastikas were removed in 1946. In 1961, however, the German authorities decided to exhume all of the remains for re-interment in a large communal ossuary located near Mont Saint-Michel in France, leaving the ground here free for local burials.

Continue along the path and leave the churchyard through the gate straight ahead. Turn right and walk along until arriving at the **St Brelade's War Memorial**. First unveiled in 1921, today it contains fifty-nine names from the two world wars and one, Sergeant Ian Harris of the Devon and Dorset Regiment, from the Troubles in Northern Ireland. In common with virtually all of Jersey's war memorials, the dead of the First World War dominate by their sheer number, reflecting the profound impact of that conflict on the island. Among them are brothers Yves and Emmanuel Boustouller, French nationals living in Jersey who were killed after recall to fight in the French Army. This family's links with Jersey remained strong after that war, however, and is sadly evidenced by the name of their nephew Louis who was killed during the Second World War while fighting with the British Army at Monte Cassino in Italy.

Leaving the memorial, turn right and walk along the main road towards the bay, taking special care because of the lack of pavement in this area. We pass in front of the St Brelade's Bay Hotel, commandeered by the Germans during the Occupation and used as a soldier's rest home, or Soldatenheim II to give its official title. For their protection, there was an air raid shelter bunker opposite and today concealed beneath the carefully tended private gardens between the road and beach. Just after passing these gardens, turn right to reach the promenade that runs above the beach.

We are in the area of *Resistance Nest Beau Rivage*, a group of German fortifications including a small bunker for a tank turret armed with a machine gun that has now largely disappeared among the developments here. We are also standing on top of a concrete anti-tank wall, designated PzM6 (*PzM standing for Panzermauern or anti-tank wall*) that was built by the Germans along the entire length of St Brelade's and Ouaisné Bays. French contractors and local labour initially carried out construction, but, after August 1942, the main workforce was Russian slave labourers who toiled here under brutal supervisors from the Organisation Todt, the construction branch of the German Army. When standing here today, particularly if the sun is shining, it is very difficult to reconcile such wanton brutality with the present circumstances, but spare a thought for those who suffered here during the Occupation.

Follow the promenade towards the promontory separating St Brelade's Bay from Ouaisné. Roughly on the site now occupied by the imposing L'Horizon Hotel was the Middle Battery, which mounted two 18-pounder cannon during the Napoleonic Wars. After crossing over the beach slip, another fortification from that period appears to our left. St Brelade's Tower No. 2 is a Conway-style round tower built in the 1780s for a garrison of one officer and ten men drawn from the Jersey Militia. On top of the tower there was a single 18-pounder cannon mounted on a carriage that allowed all round fire and which could hit a target up to one mile away.

Pass the tower and continue to walk east along the promenade until we approach the rocky promontory, called Le Grouin Point. At the end of the concrete anti-tank wall, there is a large granite wall, concave in shape and mounting four large metal rings. This structure, which probably dates from the 18th century, is the remains of a **Jersey Militia firing range**, with men shooting from the beach at a target suspended from the wall. Tucked menacingly above is a well-sited **German bunker for a 7.5cm anti-tank gun**, one of the most powerful of this type of weapon in the island and capable of firing a shell up to four and half miles. Protected by the headland, it would have presented a difficult target to destroy, while covering the beach with a devastating fire.

We have reached Le Grouin Point, formerly the location of both Napoleonic-era and other German fortifications located here as part of their *Strongpoint Le Grouin.* In 1811, **Le Grouin Battery** sat on

*German bunker for a
7.5cm anti-tank gun*

*Wartime photo of the
German bunker for a
7.5cm anti-tank gun
tucked menacingly
into Le Grouin Point
above old militia rifle
range
(CIOS collection)*

the slope above St Brelade's Bay armed with two 12-pounder cannon. Although the gun platforms are now gone, the remains of a powder magazine can be found at the top of the hill. And on the slopes at the front and sides of the promontory are numerous small German fortifications including a **searchlight shelter bunker and platform** for a 30cm searchlight on the very tip above the beach.

Our walk leads up and over the promontory following the steps and path to come down the other side into the peaceful setting of Ouaisné Bay. Near the bottom of the descent, there is a **bunker for a 4.7cm anti-tank gun** on our right, housing a weapon originally built by the Czechoslovakians, but seized by the German military during the annexation of that country prior to Second World War. Note the use of granite to camouflage the concrete above the gun mounting.

Ouaisné Tower amid the quiet setting of Ouaisné Bay

Continue until reaching the steps a short distance from the bunker that lead down to the beach. On the common away to our left is Ouaisné Tower, or **St Brelade's Tower No. 1** to give its official designation, built in the 1780s like the one found in St Brelade's Bay. Unlike that one, however, and most others remaining in Jersey, this

Conway-style round tower remains uncluttered by modern buildings or development allowing us to appreciate one of these towers in its 'natural' setting. What is not natural, of course, are the bright navigation stripes it sports today.

From here, you may want to venture towards the tower for a closer look, or continue toward the slip at the far end of Ouaisné Beach, where public toilets and options for refreshments are found. Alternatively, if the tide permits, a walk back along the beach to St Brelade is the recommended option.

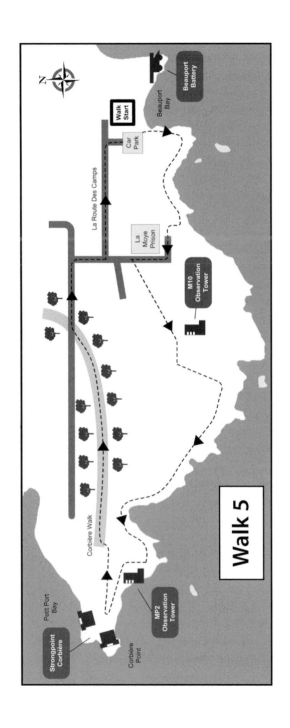

Walk 5: Rugged Outposts

A cliff-top walk from Beauport to the Corbière promontory and back via the Railway Walk.

The cliff path that winds up, down and around the rugged contours of Jersey's south-west coastline between Beauport and Corbière offers walkers exercise, breathtaking coastal views, the landmark sight of Corbière Lighthouse and a wealth of fascinating military history and fortifications. The fact it also passes some less than attractive buildings – the island's prison and desalination plant – should not detract from what is a most enjoyable, if at times challenging, Jersey war walk.

Start:	Public car park above Beauport Bay
Length:	4 miles / 3 hours
Difficulty:	Challenging with some steep ascents and descents on cliff paths
Getting there –	
By car:	free parking in the car park above Beauport Bay
By bus:	Route 12 goes from Liberation Station to Corbière. Alight at a stop on Route du Sud and walk down La Route Des Camps to reach Beauport Car Park.
Refreshments:	Restaurant and bar at Corbière
Amenities:	Public toilets at Corbière

From the car park, follow the path leading to the beach, but turn immediately right passing the green pumping station box to reach the cliff top above Beauport Bay and a magnificent view over the beach below. On the opposite side of the bay, in the headland above the beach, there are some structures visible among the rocks and greenery. These are the remains of **Beauport Battery**, one of several batteries built to protect St Brelade's Bay that lies beyond and which during the Napoleonic Wars mounted two 24-pounder cannon. During the Occupation, the Germans added their own defence in the form of a 7.5cm gun, a 3.7cm anti-tank gun and **bunker for a tank turret** armed with a machine gun, the emplacements for which are on private land today and therefore not possible to visit.

Leaving the bay, continue on the footpath which meanders through the gorse, splitting at times into different directions, although marker stones do indicate which route is the coastal path. Turning left at any junction typically takes you closer to the cliff edge before returning to the main path, but avoid turning right into the fields. After a while, the path drops steeply down and climbs steeply back up again, with steps cut to help the descent and ascent. Upon reaching the top at the other side, a small but impressive concrete **gun emplacement** soon appears to our left.

During the Occupation, this emplacement housed a German four-barrelled 2cm anti-aircraft gun, called a Flakvierling, one of the most effective anti-aircraft weapons in the island. The one here was part of the defences of **Battery Roon**, the heaviest German artillery battery

Emplacement for a four barrelled 2cm anti-aircraft gun on the coastal path, once used to defend the nearby Battery Roon

in Jersey. Its four 22cm guns were located a short distance away from here on land now mostly covered by the modern day HM Prison Le Moye and a nearby housing estate. It means that little of Battery Roon remains to be seen today, although one of the gun emplacements is now a garden feature of La Place Le Boutillier housing estate.

Continuing from the cliff top emplacement, the path takes us around the unsightly prison perimeter to reach a tarmac road near a house called **HM Old Signal Point**. This location was one of ten signal stations established in the late 18th century to provide an early warning system against approaching enemy vessels. With each station in sight of two others, it was possible to relay information swiftly around the island and even pass on to Guernsey by means of a station on the north-west tip of Jersey.

Take the tarmac road around the prison until reaching a left pointing sign indicating the coastal path once more. Follow this towards the modern tower that appears to have a large golf ball on top, but which actually houses an airport weather radar. While approaching the radar station, however, above the gorse on our left appears a monolithic concrete structure, this one covered in all manner of aerials and antennae.

This is M10 (*M standing for Meßstelle or Range-finding Position*), a German **artillery range-finding bunker** built during the Occupation

German artillery range-finding bunker M10 in its wartime camouflage
(Société Jersiaise)

to resemble a house, complete with a false pitched roof. The front of this building has viewing slits from where artillery controllers would have directed fire on vessels off Jersey's south coast while nearby there are two personnel shelter bunkers. Today it is used by the Jersey Amateur Radio Society and cannot be approached without permission.

Leaving M10 behind us, continue on the path, which skirts the radar tower before turning toward the cliff edge once again. Away to the left, a split-level concrete structure appears across a small valley. This is **M10a**, another German **artillery range-finding bunker**, located on private land. Turning right, we follow the cliff path as it winds around and up and down a number of rocky bays and headlands. Here and there are the remains of granite buildings to remind us of the quarries once worked here, while some way along the coast we pass the large and much more modern desalination plant for those times when the island's water supply runs low. The coastal path descends here, before rising again next to a set of rails running down to a granite building associated with the plant. Climb up beside them to rejoin the path next to a locked metal gate. After climbing a little more we reach a roofed granite oblong building, which is a **19th century explosives store for a nearby quarry**.

Continue on the path, heading now towards the concrete tower ahead. After a few more ups and downs, the path arrives at the base of MP2 (*MP standing for Marinepeilstände und Meßstellen or Naval Coastal Artillery Direction and Range-finding Position*), one of three huge **naval observation towers** constructed by the Germans during the Occupation. The original intention was to build nine of these towers around the coast, each capable of directing artillery fire at naval targets approaching or passing the island, although only three were completed. Having served as a radio tower after the Occupation, today this one is a unique holiday let run by Jersey Heritage. Near its base we find a partially buried **personnel shelter bunker** complete with periscope tube on its roof and a small **one man bunker** closer to the cliff edge.

*Naval Observation Tower MP2, one of nine planned for
Jersey of which only three were ever completed.*

Turning our back on the bunkers, take the road that runs past
the Corbière Phare Apartments and Restaurant, a welcome place for
lunch or a drink, and turn left at the main road to descend down
past the public toilets towards Corbière point. On our right, rising
from the higher ground, there is a another German **artillery range-
finding bunker**, this one designated M1 and marked out today in
bright navigation colours. A little further still on the same side there
is a one man bunker near a now largely buried **personnel shelter
bunker**. Cross the main road at this point, and take the access road
leading down towards the lighthouse to visit more fortifications of
Strongpoint Corbière.

Searchlight bunker above the lower car park at Corbière

During the Occupation, the Germans decided to make Corbière one of the most strongly fortified places in Jersey. Given its important position covering the south coast approaches to St Helier and flanking the wide sandy St Ouen's Bay to the north, it is easy to see why. As we walk down the road towards the lighthouse, we will consider the fortifications on each side.

From the edge of the car park at the top of the road, we can look over to see a **bunker for a 10.5cm gun** situated to cover the Petit Port Bay beyond. Today it is in the care of the Channel Islands Occupation Society (CIOS), fully preserved and still containing its original armament. To visit, there is a path down that starts on the road below the car park. Moving on down the road towards the lighthouse, we pass a small **machine gun emplacement** on the left and, on the right, a **heavy machine gun bunker** that once had a massive steel turret on top armed with two machine guns. Although the turret has long since fallen victim to the post-war scrap drive, the bunker is under restoration by the CIOS as is the next one on our right, a **bunker for an M19 mortar**. This fortification, which is unique in Jersey, once contained a weapon capable of firing 120 mortar bombs per minute up to a maximum range of 750 metres. After the war, the mortar and its steel turret were removed with the aid of explosives, leaving the damage to the concrete seen today. The CIOS have undertaken a remarkable restoration, however, including re-fabricating the mortar turret and its weapon. Both bunkers are open for visitors at times during the summer together with the remarkable underground passage that connects them. Continue on past another **small machine gun emplacement** on the other side of the road to reach the lower car park on the left, which is actually the roof of a second bunker for a **10.5cm gun**, although this one no longer has its weapon. Above the car park sits a **searchlight shelter bunker** once housing a 60cm searchlight that would emerge onto either of the two platforms in front to illuminate targets at night.

After visiting this last bunker, we retrace our steps back up the lighthouse access road and along the main road until reaching the public toilets on the right. Opposite them we find the start (or end) of the Railway Walk, or Corbière Walk as it is now called. Take this, passing the former Corbière Station, now a house modernised by the addition of glass atriums. Prior to the Occupation, this was the route for the Jersey Western Railway, which ran from St Helier to St Aubin and then on to here at Corbière. Declining business meant its closure in 1936, although the former route remained for re-use by the Germans who laid a metre-gauge track to provide transport for their mass of building materials.

Continue along the railway walk until it is cut by the first main road. Turn right here and carefully follow the road until reaching the junction with Route du Sud and a signpost pointing out Beauport Bay. There is a bus stop here, which can be used to return to St Helier, or we can turn right onto Rue du Sud and then, after 100 metres, left onto La Route Des Camps and a walk back to our start at Beauport Bay Car Park.

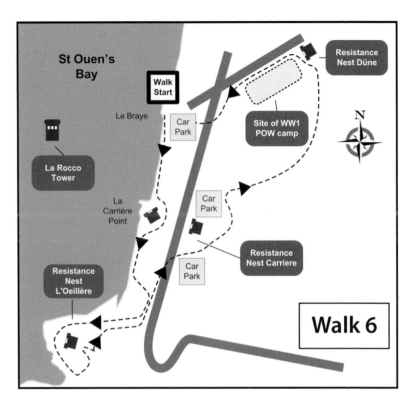

German personnel shelter bunker in the dunes near Le Braye Slip

Walk 6: Killing Time

A seashore ramble from Le Braye to L'Oeillière Headland and back across the dunes to visit forgotten prisoner-of-war camp.

The dunes that fill much of the south of St Ouen's Bay are an important open space and conservation area today, strongly protected against any development. Of course wartime necessities tended to ignore such conventions, especially given how vulnerable the beach here, and the area immediately behind, is to an attack from the sea, and so over the centuries there has been plenty of defensive developments as a consequence. On this seashore and sand dune walk, we visit many of these defences, and the locations of others now lost to the seas and forgotten. We also visit another largely forgotten military installation – although one designed to keep the enemy in, rather than out.

Start:	Le Braye Slip Car Park
Length:	2.5 miles / 2 hours
Difficulty:	Moderate: two steep ascents / descents that can be bypassed if necessary
Getting there –	
By car:	Free parking at Le Braye Slip
By bus:	Route 12, alighting at le Braye Slip
Refreshments:	Café at Le Braye and bar / eating house at La Pulente
Amenities:	Public toilets at Le Braye and La Pulente

From the car park, walk down towards the slip leading to the beach. On the right, a bunker entrance appears, the first of several in this area that formed *Resistance Nest Les Brayes*, created by the Germans to defend this part of St Ouen's Bay. This was a **bunker for a 4.7cm anti-tank gun**, angled to fire north along the beach, while on the left at the top of the slip is a **garage-type bunker** that today is home to deck chairs but during the Occupation protected a mobile 3.7cm anti-tank gun. On either side of the slip, partially set into the walls, are some examples of early German defences – rudimentary **bunkers for machine guns**, some of which once had thick metal plates on top. In addition to those immediately around the slip, the defences here included two personnel shelter bunkers, which are visible among the dunes next to the main road, and a **water pumping and storage bunker** that is now lost under the sands.

While standing here at the top of the slip, it's a good time to consider the most famous fortification in St Ouen's Bay, which lies half a mile out to sea. **La Rocco Tower**, which was originally called Gordon's Tower, was built on a rocky outcrop in 1801. It was the twenty-third and last of the Conway-style Jersey round towers, and the most impressive – in both appearance and armament. As well as mounting one cannon on top, the protected gun platform around the tower accommodated four 32-pounder cannon, creating a formidable advanced defence for the whole bay. Damaged during the Occupation, it lay partially ruined for many years and in danger of loss to the sea until a campaign in the late 1960s persuaded Jersey's government to pay for its restoration. Given the amount of times La Rocco Tower has appeared in tourism promotions since, it was money well spent.

La Rocco Tower was not the only Conway-style round tower in St Ouen's Bay however. Along the shore were four others, constructed about ten years earlier amid the dunes overlooking the beach. The closeness to the shoreline proved to be the downfall of three of them, however, including the second of the four, called **Tower B, or Tour de la Pierre Buttée**, which once stood here at Le Braye. Although originally constructed some way back from the beach, tidal erosion undermined its foundations and eventually caused the tower to collapse.

Continuing our walk, climb up to the left at the top of the slip to follow the sandy footpath running behind the seawall, which is actually a German **anti-tank wall** designated PzM4 (*PzM standing for Panzermauern or anti-tank wall*) and built in 1941. While it may have never had its ability to stop Allied tanks tested, it has proved useful since in halting the coastal erosion that brought down the tower at Le Braye and also the one that once stood near La Carrière Point now visible in front of us.

Left: Ex-French 10.5cm gun still found in a bunker at La Carrière Point
Right: The remains of Tower A, or Tour Du Sud, before it was finally lost to the seas
(Société Jersiaise)

The **Tower A, or Tour du Sud**, was the first of the four Conway-style round towers in the bay, and like its counterpart lost to coastal erosion, although in this case not until the early years of the 20th century. This was also the location of *Resistance Nest Carrière*, the German group of fortifications responsible for defending this part of the bay. The first of these is immediately ahead of us as we walk along above the seawall, a **bunker for a 10.5cm gun** that, unlike most of its counterparts, still contains an original weapon. The Germans brought thirty-four of these guns to Jersey during the Occupation, having taken them from the French Army after the fall of France in June 1940. The guns, which date back to the First World War, were originally mounted on wheeled carriages, although the majority were converted on arrival in Jersey to operate from bunkers such as this one. Most disappeared during post-war scrap drives, with only a few surviving beyond the 1950s. This one was originally located at Rozel Fort before recovery by the Channel Islands Occupation Society (CIOS) and eventual placement as an impressive addition to this bunker. Its presence helps remind us of the potency of these fortifications. With a range of just over seven miles, it would have dominated the beach in front with high-explosive shells, its fire interlocking with others to create a vast killing field for anyone attempting to land here.

Climbing up and around the bunker, to our left on the roadside is a small **one man bunker** while to the right is a **bunker for a 4.7cm anti-tank gun** facing south along the beach. This one, which has granite set around the gun mounting as camouflage, is also in the care of the CIOS and may be open to the public from time to time. Also part of the German defences here are a number of other fortifications on the hill across the road, which we will visit later on the walk, but for now, we continue along the bay on top of another **German anti-tank wall**, this one designated PzM5. Continue until reaching the La Pulente public toilets, at which point we climb up to follow the path alongside the main road, passing a small **bunker for a tank turret** on the right opposite the pub here.

Turn right on reaching the footpath going round the L'Oeillière Headland and follow it until arriving at a complex of bunkers, part of a group of German defences called *Resistance Nest L'Oeilliere*. It consisted of a **bunker for a 10.5cm gun** of the right and a **bunker for a 4.7cm anti-tank gun** on the left, with a single entrance below and to the right of the path. Completing the defence was a **tank-turret armed with a machine gun** that sat on top and between both. From here we can see the interlocking design of the German defences, with the bunker for the 10.5cm gun facing towards the bunker for a 4.7cm anti-tank gun just visited at La Carrière, while the bunker for the 4.7cm anti-tank gun here faces in the opposite direction towards Corbière Point and a bunker there that faces back towards us. Anyone trying to land would have faced fire from at least two sides, while each group of bunkers provided mutual support for its neighbours.

Leaving the bunkers, continue on the path around the headland towards quiet Petit Port Bay. Before this, however, a wooden marker indicates a left turn to a path up and over the headland, which we take unless you would prefer to remain on the flat by retracing your steps back round to the start of the path. At the top of the climb, there is a double set of wooden stile gates. After passing the first one, turn left and walk towards the front of the headland where as well as fantastic views over the entire bay, we find a German **artillery observation bunker**. This was the forward command post for **Battery Ziethen**, an artillery unit armed with four 7.7cm guns situated where the houses behind the headland stand today.

Return to the path, and descend left to reach the start of the headland walk once more. From here we retrace our steps back to La Pulente toilets, but from there remain on the roadside footpath until arriving opposite the public car park on the other side of the road. Cross and find a path that leads from the car park into the dunes, running left towards the broad sandy path rising up the promontory here. Again, if you would prefer not to climb, walk around the base of the promontory to re-join on the other side. As we begin to climb, note the small one-man bunker on the right, part of Resistance Nest Carrière, to which we have now returned.

On reaching the top of the sandy path, those with energy can continue up to the right and visit a small German **artillery observation bunker**, before beginning the descent down the other side. Below on the right is another small **one man bunker** while on the left is a more substantial construction. This is a **searchlight shelter bunker**, complete with the remains of a concrete ramp to wheel the 60cm searchlight up to a **concrete platform** overlooking La Carrière Point from where it could have illuminated targets in the bay during the night time.

Having inspected the fortifications here, walk down to the large car park below and cross it to take the exit path more or less opposite onto the dunes. The dunes and grasslands here are a protected site of special scientific interest and maintained against erosion or overuse, meaning the many paths criss-crossing the area are only the faintest of tracks. The next point of interest on our walk is on the other side of this flat area, at the end of a line of higher dunes that circle around. The path generally goes in that direction, but to remain fixed, observe the lights and barriers on the high ground in the distance that mark the end of the airport runway and use that as a bearing. After a while we pass a few large bushes on the left, beyond which we climb to the summit of the dune nearest the road to find the remains of the German *Resistance Nest Düne*.

The fortification we are now on top of was a **heavy machine gun bunker** armed with two machine guns in a huge steel turret. The turret, which would have defended the road out of the bay as part of the German second line of defence, was removed in an early 1950s scrap drive leaving the damage seen today. In support were two mobile 7.5cm anti-tank guns housed in garage-type bunkers with ramps running up to **concrete emplacements** from where they would fire in the event of an attack. One of these lies half-buried a short distance away from this bunker, with the platform visible on edge of the dune, while the second was on the other side of the road and now lost in the sand quarry. A **water pumping and storage bunker** also lies buried nearby.

This location is a good place to consider the final point of interest on this walk. In 1914, the British War Office ordered the construction of a prisoner-of-war camp in Jersey, and the land between this bunker and La Braye was chosen. **Blanches Banques POW Camp** opened in 1915 to hold more than fifteen hundred German prisoners of war who remained until 1917 when they left to work in England. In 1918, a further one thousand prisoners arrived, with some remaining until October 1919. While the camp regime does not appear to have been overly harsh, with sports, recreation and musical concerts to fill the days, some of the inmates were not happy just killing time but determined to escape. Two tunnels were dug, out from the camp under the road now visible to the right. One was discovered before use, but six men escaped through the other only to be caught not too far away in St Brelade's Bay. While admiring their ingenuity and effort, it's not clear just how they planned to get off the island once out.

The camp was demolished after the war, with the site returned to nature. From this vantage point it is possible to make out its general layout, however, with the guards' quarters closest to where we are now, and the prisoner's huts running down in rows of four at right angles to the road. In between were the ablution blocks. The foundations of the more substantial buildings can be visited on our way back to Le Braye where our walk ends, together with other humps and bumps discernible among the grass.

Blanches Banques POW Camp looking down from the dune that later became the heart of the Germans' Resistance Nest Düne (Société Jersiaise)

Wartime photo of the heavy machine gun bunker complete with its steel turret that formed the key defence of the Germans' Resistance Nest Düne (CIOS collection)

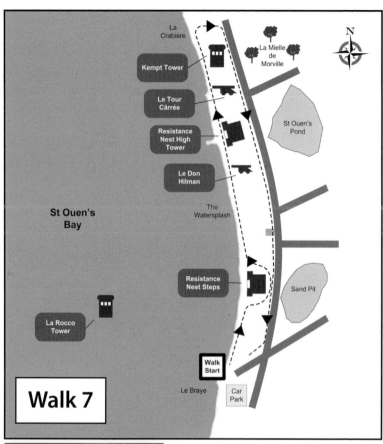

Walk 7

La Crabière

Kempt Tower

Le Tour Cârrée

Resistance Nest High Tower

Le Don Hilman

Resistance Nest Steps

La Rocco Tower

St Ouen's Bay

The Watersplash

Le Braye

Walk Start

Car Park

La Mielle de Morville

St Ouen's Pond

Sand Pit

N

Opposite top: Kempt Tower, built in the 1830s, but used in both the First and Second World Wars

Left: George Carteret who unsuccessfully defended St Ouen's Bay against the Parliamentarian forces in 1651

Walk 7: Centre of Attention

A long but easy-going stroll along the fortified middle of St Ouen's Bay from Le Braye to Le Crabière and back again.

Anyone planning to invade Jersey in years gone by would certainly have had St Ouen's Bay high on the list of promising locations to start. And high on the list of possible landing places would have been the centre of the bay, away from the reefs and high ground that dominate either end, and with a wide hinterland behind the beach to assemble forces before pressing on inland. With this in mind, it is obvious why an invading force did indeed land here in 1651, to defeat local troops before moving on to eventually capture the whole island. It's also obvious why in the centuries that followed, successive generations of defenders built the many fortifications we pass on this pleasant and very interesting seafront walk.

Start:	Le Braye Slip Car Park
Length:	4 miles / 3 hours
Difficulty:	Easy
Getting there –	
By car:	Free parking at Le Braye
By bus:	Route 12, alighting at Le Braye Slip
Refreshments:	Several refreshment options en-route
Amenities:	Public toilets at La Braye

Leaving the car park, pass behind the café at Le Braye to take the path running north along the top of the seawall. Like most others in the bay, this wall is actually a German **anti-tank wall**, designated PzM3 (*PzM standing for Panzermauern or anti-tank wall*), and built for the obvious purpose of preventing an enemy invader gaining an easy exit from the beach. Since the Occupation, it has proved something of a liability, however, with continual efforts made to reinforce and underpin its foundations. Unlike in some other areas of the bay, the sea regularly reaches the wall here and is the cause of most of the damage. Another possible source of weakness is because of those who built it. Many young local men who broke German rules during the early years of the Occupation were sent to work on the construction of this wall, and reportedly took every opportunity to weaken its structure by contaminating the freshly poured cement.

The purpose of maintaining the wall is to protect the coast against tidal erosion, a force that up until the Occupation scoured the dunes along the shore. A victim of this erosion was a Conway-style round tower built among the dunes about six hundred metres north of Le Braye Slip. Called **Tower C**, it was the third of four built along the shoreline at the end of the 18th century, but was undermined and lost to the sea within a hundred years. Another lost Napoleonic Wars era fortification here was the **Half-Moon Battery**, situated between Le Braye and the C Tower, which mounted three 24-pounder cannon manned by members of the Jersey Militia in times of threat.

The building of these and many other fortifications followed an attempted landing in St Ouen's Bay by a French force in 1779. While that had been unsuccessful, it served as a salutatory reminder of how vulnerable this part of the island was to invasion, although the defenders should have been aware of this because of a successful landing here over a hundred years earlier during the English Civil War.

After the defeat of Charles II at the Battle of Worcester in 1651, Jersey was almost the last Royalist stronghold in the British Isles and a base from which privateers raided Parliamentarian shipping in the Channel. Determined to end to this, a **Parliamentarian force arrived in St Ouen's Bay** in October 1651 to take the island. Defending Jersey was George Carteret, who marched his force of Royalist soldiers and

Jersey Militia into the bay to defeat the first attempt at a landing. The invaders were not put off, however, and after sailing back and forth for a while to confuse and tire Carteret's men, landed again, most probably in this central part of the bay, this time to defeat the local forces, many of whom were less than enthusiastic about dying for the Royalist cause. George Carteret escaped the battle, however, fleeing to Elizabeth Castle for a siege that ended with capitulation in December that year.

During the Occupation, the Germans were quick to recognise the vulnerability of St Ouen's Bay and began building fortifications here soon after their arrival in June 1940. At first these defensive works were rudimentary affairs, partially built with materials to hand. Soon more permanent work commenced, and a series of designated 'Strongpoints', 'Resistance Nests' and the lesser 'Operational Positions' appeared as clusters of bunkers often built around a former beach slipway or existing earlier fortification. At El Tico Café, which we arrive at next, was Resistance Nest Steps Punkt 43, named after map features rather than the usual practice of choosing a local landmark.

Just before the café, which commands magnificent views over the bay, is a vegetation-covered bank to the right of the path that conceals the remains of a **heavy machine gun bunker** once topped by a huge steel turret housing two machine guns. Although scrap men removed the

The shorn off remains of a heavy machine gun bunker turret just before reaching El Tico Café

turret in the early 1950s, its base remains to show just how thick the steel turret was. At the café, turn right to enter its car park where we find a **water pumping and storage bunker,** once used to provide fresh water to the Resistance Nest defenders, but today making an excellent advertising hoarding. Turn left at this bunker and leave the car park to reach the track leading up to the lifeguard station next to the café, noting a **personnel shelter bunker** on its left, and **one man bunker** on the right. Follow the track up to a large **searchlight shelter bunker**, from which the remains of a concrete ramp leads up to a concrete emplacement with a curious base for the 60cm searchlight used here to illuminate targets during the night time. In front is a **bunker for a 10.5cm gun** angled to fire north along the beach.

From this last bunker, we can resume our walk along the wall, passing the little access road at Le Port before arriving at the Watersplash, location of the German *Operational Position Bucht*. This was one of their earliest defended locations in the bay, fortified with some minor **mortar and machine gun bunkers** visible beside the footpath just before reaching the modern day building.

Pressing on along the bay, we soon reach one its most iconic buildings, a small white-painted structure now owned by the National Trust for Jersey and named **Le Don Hilton**, or La Caumine à Marie Best. It dates back to the mid-17th century at least, when it was the St Peter's Guard House and Magazine, while by the Napoleonic Wars, it had become part of the **Middle Battery**, located here and armed with three 24-pounder cannon. Today it is available for hire as accommodation that is rudimentary enough to allow a taste of life as a soldier here more than two hundred years ago.

Continuing our walk, we arrive next at Big Vern's Café with its associated apartments, shops and surf school. Before the Occupation, this was the site of the last of the four Conway-style round towers standing on the shores of the bay, and the only one not to fall victim to coastal erosion. But the Germans decided to demolish the **Tower D,** or **High Tower**, when

Le Don Hilton, once part of the Napoleonic Wars era Middle Battery

building their fortifications here to create *Resistance Nest High Tower*, which was responsible for defending this part of the bay. There were two **bunkers for 4.7cm anti-tank guns**, back to back, with one directly in front of the café angled to fire south and the other built to block the pre-war slipway and angled to fire north along the beach. Furthermore, to prevent any invaders using the slip, it had metal girders inserted and cemented in place. After the Occupation, the north-facing bunker was mostly demolished in order to reopen the slip and little now remains, while the metal girders were cut down to surface level, leaving the traces visible today. A little way past the slip is a **bunker for a 10.5cm gun**, while in between are the remains of **earlier German bunkers**, including the **mounting for a gun** in the beachside car park.

Leaving Big Vern's, we walk on for a further 300 metres to reach the next important fortification in the bay. **Le Tour Cârrée**, or square tower, which dates back to the 18th century, although earlier defensive works may have existed on this site. By the time of the Napoleonic Wars, the guardhouse and magazine had become part of the **North Battery**, which mounted three 24-pounder cannon on a platform in front, while in the years that followed it was remodelled into a mini-fort, or blockhouse, capable of all-round defence. Today, it is another of Jersey Heritage's holiday lets, and prominently marked with navigation strips making it difficult to miss.

Continuing on, we next approach **Kempt Tower**, one of three towers built in the bay during the 1830s following increased tensions between Britain and France. Unlike the original and far more numerous Conway-style round towers built elsewhere in the island, these new fortifications were true 'martello towers', very similar in design to those found along the south coast of England. On its top was a 24-pounder cannon, with accommodation for crew and ammunition below, while on a granite platform still found in front of the tower stood a further three 24-pounder cannons, making this a formidable defensive strongpoint during the 19th century. By the start of the 20th century, however, Kempt Tower was no longer in use, although it did enjoy a brief renaissance during the First World War when the Jersey Militia used it and other fortifications along the coast as bases for defending the bay against enemy landings.

Early German fortifications near Kempt Tower, with an interesting use of local materials

During the Occupation, the Germans rearmed Kempt Tower as part of *Resistance Nest Kempt Tower*, rebuilding the internal floors, creating loopholes to fire through and placing a twin machine gun on the roof. In the land around, they built some rudimentary **early fortifications** in 1941, which we pass just before arriving at the tower, and **searchlight shelter bunker** with **concrete emplacement** beyond, which today supports the rather odd-looking beach house. There are further bunkers behind the tower, which we see on our return walk, but for now press on past the large **bunker for a 10.5cm gun**. Adjoining the latter, which is angled to fire south, is a covered concrete ramp leading down an unusual **machine gun bunker** built into the anti-tank wall here.

Our final point of interest on this walk is found about a thousand metres further along the seafront where a cluster of fortifications forms the German's *Resistance Nest La Crabière*. Prior to the Occupation, a granite slipway led down to the beach here, built to assist farmers collecting seaweed from the beaches for use as a natural fertiliser. To prevent its use by invaders attempting to leave the beach, the Germans not only removed the slip to the beach, but blocked the top by constructing a large fortification consisting of **two bunkers for 4.7cm anti-tank guns,** one angled south, the other north. Also constructed here was a **water pumping and storage bunker,** lying inland near the main road.

From La Crabière we turn inland to walk along the main road back to Le Braye, passing some rearward elements of the defensive positions already visited. As an alternative, you may want to consider continuing north from this point to Les Laveurs Slip to visit the excellent CI Military Museum, which is covered in detail on Walk 8.

On the way back to Kempt Tower, note the entrances on the opposite side of the road to La Mielle de Morville, one of Jersey's most important nature reserves, which includes a number of marked paths and walkways. Once approaching the tower, on the right we can see some of the German built fortifications, including a water pumping and storage bunker, although access to them is fenced off, while half buried in the car park on the other side of the road is a personnel shelter bunker. Another personnel shelter bunker is on the right next to the footpath around a hundred metres beyond the tower. Pressing on, we pass Le Tour Cârrée, behind which is St Ouen's Pond, Jersey's largest natural body of fresh water. During the Occupation, the Germans dug two huge anti-tank ditches on either side, to impede any attackers who managed to breach the first line of defence along the beach. The National Trust for Jersey Wetland Centre is passed on the opposite side of the road. This superb facility for observing birds on the pond incorporates a **personnel shelter bunker,** restored and used as a classroom on occasion. Beyond the Discovery Bay Apartments is a **water pumping and storage bunker** on this side. Further on again, at the Watersplash, a **personnel shelter bunker** lurks beneath the decorative water feature along the roadside. Thereafter, the footpath takes us back past El Tico, and its fortifications, and on to Le Braye Slip where our walk ends.

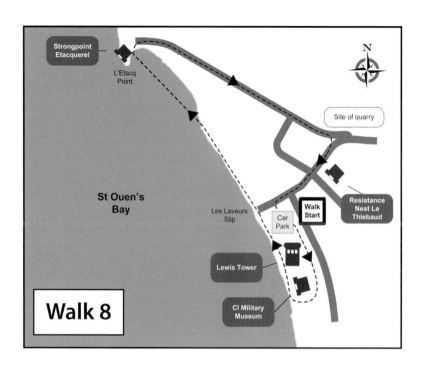

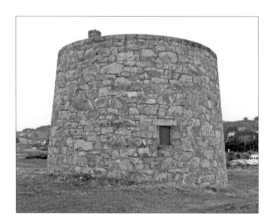

Lewis Tower, built in the 1830s and modified by the Germans during the Occupation

Walk 8: On the Quiet Side

A walk around the north of St Ouen's Bay from Lewis Tower to L'Etacq and back again.

The northern end of St Ouen's Bay is undoubtedly its quieter part, where in places it can feel as though you have stepped back to a time when agriculture prevailed and the seashore was the undisturbed domain of fishermen. This quietness resulted in a lower level of fortification than elsewhere, although an attempted invasion here in 1779 serves to remind that no part of the bay was secure from attack.

Start:	Les Laveurs Slip Car Park
Length:	2.5 miles / 2 hours
Difficulty:	Easy
Getting there –	
By car:	Free parking in Les Laveurs Slip, which is opposite Jersey Pearl on the Five Mile Road
By bus:	Route 12 from Liberation Station, alighting at Jersey Pearl to cross road to car park
Refreshments:	Jersey Pearl near Les Laveurs Slip
Amenities:	Public toilets at Les Laveurs Slip

From the car park, we walk first to **Lewis Tower**, standing a short distance away across the grass. The tower was one of five built in Jersey during the 1830s at a time of renewed tensions between Britain and France. In contrast to the original and far more numerous Conway-style round towers already in the island and Portelet Tower, Noirmont Tower and Icho Tower built during the Napoleonic Wars, these new fortifications were true 'martello towers', like those found along the south coast of England. When completed in 1834 Lewis Tower mounted one 32-pounder cannon on top, with accommodation for one officer and eighteen men inside. During the Occupation, the Germans added the adjoining concrete **garage-type bunker** to protect a mobile 3.7cm anti-tank gun, placed twin machine guns on top and created a ready-made personnel shelter by opening a door in the tower's base and reconstructing the interior.

Lewis Tower is on or near the site of an earlier fortification called **Du Parcq's Battery**, which stood here during the Napoleonic Wars armed with three cannon. It took its name from the Rector of St Ouen, Le Sire du Parcq, who decisively placed the cannon of the Jersey Militia here during an **attempted French invasion in 1779**, two years before the Battle of Jersey. On this occasion a large French force under the command of the Prince of Nassau set out to land in Jersey, but uncooperative weather forced them round the island in full sight of its defenders, who hurried from place to place in order to resist. At last, the French ships arrived here in St Ouen's Bay but, with the tide going out, the captains of the larger warships were unwilling to risk coming too close to shore, while those commanding the smaller transports could not land in the face of the Militia cannon. After a standoff, the sorry French fleet returned home, while the island celebrated.

During the Occupation, the Germans incorporated Lewis Tower into *Resistance Nest Lewis Tower*, which was responsible for the defence of this area. A key part of that defence was the nearby **bunker for a 10.5cm gun**, now home to the **Channel Islands Military Museum**. The museum, which is worthy of a visit now or at the end of our walk, holds an extraordinary collection of Occupation memorabilia and military equipment, while outside are seen examples of German anti-tank obstacles once commonplace along the island's shoreline. Climbing on top, we find a small **tank turret**, typical of numerous

An ex-French tank turret situated on the Channel Islands Military Museum, one of the few remaining turrets of the many brought to Jersey

such examples installed by the Germans, having captured them from the French Army after the fall of France in June 1940. While most disappeared to the scrap men in the 1950s, a few remained in less accessible places, including this one that was originally at St Aubin's Fort. From here, some of the other German fortifications are visible, including a nearby **searchlight shelter bunker**. The resistance nest also possessed two **personnel shelter bunkers,** which today are across the road among the trees, while a **water pumping and storage bunker bunker** stood until 2015, when demolished during the building of the new luxury houses here.

Leaving the bunker, walk along the seawall, the top of which was added during the Occupation as an **anti-tank defence**, to reach a **bunker for a 4.7cm anti-tank gun** that once covered the beach north from here. The gun, together with half the bunker, are now gone as we discover after climbing down onto the slip, removed after 1945 in order to reopen access to the beach.

At this point, our walk continues across the beach or along the top of the seawall to L'Etacq Point, which is visible below the headland at the end of the beach. Between here and L'Etacq, there are no fortifications to visit, although we do pass 'Le Petit Fort', a granite house built in the early 20th century with ramparts and loopholes to resemble something earlier. On reaching L'Etacq, walk up the slip and turn left to view the huge German bunker on the rocky promontory.

Prior to the Occupation, L'Etacq Tower sat on these rocks, built in the 1830s like Lewis Tower and to the same design. This strategic point was too valuable for the Germans, however, and in 1942, they demolished L'Etacq Tower to build a fortification of their own. This bunker was a key part of *Strongpoint Etacquerel*, which was responsible for the defences in this part of the bay, and is effectively two joined fortifications, a **bunker for a 10.5cm gun** on the right and a **heavy machine gun bunker** on the left that once mounted a huge steel turret on top. Both gun and turret disappeared in a post-Occupation scrap drive, while the bunkers are now home to seawater tanks and cold storage for a fish merchant.

L'Etacq Tower before its destruction by the Germans during the Occupation
(Société Jersiaise)

Leaving the bunkers, walk back past the slip on our right to follow Route Des Harves, noting the **small early German concrete fortification** above the road to our left, and the larger one a short distance further on. This second **bunker for a 10.5cm gun** is angled to fire south along the beach, and with its range of just over seven miles is able to cover the whole length of St Ouen's Bay. Behind it there is an extensive tunnel system which links to an entrance on the hill above, near which stood a 60cm searchlight for illuminating targets at night.

Leaving L'Etacq, walk along the road that soon joins La Route de l'Etacq, noting the concentration of potato fields here. These west-facing slopes, which may be covered in polythene to nurture and protect their crop, are among the earliest to produce the famous Jersey Royal potatoes for the market, so the effort put into cultivation can be well rewarded. In due course, the road forks where a sign announces 1855, and we follow the left hand or upper road until reaching a car park on the right. During the Occupation, the quarries on either side of the valley here were vital for producing the aggregate needed by the Germans to build their fortifications. The car park was formerly the site of a huge stone crusher imported from Germany; it was serviced by a mixture of skilled overseers and forced and slave labour, mostly Spaniards and Russians who were housed in a camp in St Ouen's Bay.

German bunker for a 10.5cm gun backing onto L'Etacq Headland behind which an extensive tunnel complex exists

Walk through the car park to arrive at another main road where we turn right, passing the remains of quarrying installations on the left, until reaching a crossroads where Rue Des Pres joins on the right-hand side. Hidden in the undergrowth on the opposite side of the road here are the remains of the *Resistance Nest La Thiebaud*, which defended the road out of the bay as part of the German second line of defence. Among its fortifications was a **heavy machine gun bunker** with huge steel turret to dominate the road, although scrap men removed the turret during the 1950s. There was also a **garage-type bunker** for protecting a mobile 7.5cm anti-tank gun and a mobile 3.7cm anti-tank gun, which in time of attack would run out onto concrete emplacements, and a **searchlight shelter bunker** and **platform** for a 60cm searchlight.

Leaving the crossroad, continue along the road to Les Laveurs Slip where our walk ends.

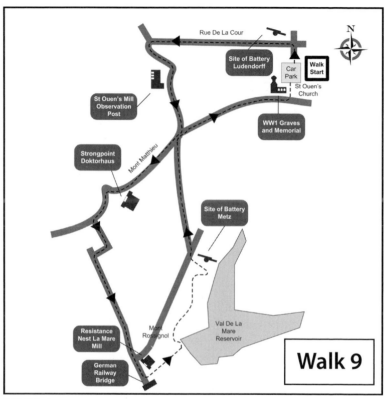

Rue De La Cour

Site of Battery Ludendorff

Car Park

Walk Start

St Ouen's Church

St Ouen's Mill Observation Post

WW1 Graves and Memorial

Strongpoint Doktorhaus

Mont Mathieu

Site of Battery Metz

Resistance Nest La Mare Mill

Mont Rossignol

Val De La Mare Reservoir

German Railway Bridge

Walk 9

N

Left: Le Mare Mill complete with German observation post addition on top

Opposite top: Camouflaged heavy machine gun turret, the centrepiece of Resistance Le Mare Mill

Walk 9: Defence in Depth

A circular walk from St Ouen's Church through the German second line defences of St Ouen's Bay and their heavy guns behind.

Nowhere in the Island do you find a higher concentration of German fortifications than in St Ouen's Bay. Here the occupiers not only constructed an immensely strong defensive line to halt invaders on the beach, but also created a second line of fortifications to prevent any attackers reaching the high ground surrounding the bay. On this panoramic walk, we visit some impressive remains of this second line of fortifications, together with those of nearby artillery positions, which added to the bay's defence in depth. Our walk also takes in the tranquil setting of St Ouen's Church to recall the tragic impact of earlier conflicts in Jersey and some of its oldest families.

Start:	St Ouen's Church Car Park
Length:	3 miles / 2.5 hours
Difficulty:	Moderate: one steep ascent on a footpath
Getting there –	
By car:	Free parking at St Ouen's Church
By bus:	Take Route 9 from Liberation Station to St Ouen's Village, alighting outside St Ouen's Manor and walk down Rue du Manoir to reach the church
Refreshments:	None en route
Amenities:	Toilets in St Ouen's Church Car Park

Leave the church car park via its access road (we visit the church at the end of the walk), and walk the short distance to the crossroads where we turn left into Rue de la Cour. Within a few metres there is a raised area of ground on the right and the occasional lump of concrete visible in the fields here and among the undergrowth. Stop for a moment.

The German's **Battery Ludendorff** once filled the fields to the right of the road here, equipped with three 21cm heavy guns capable of firing at targets up to ten miles away. The **emplacements** for the guns were less substantial than those at Noirmont or Les Landes, and are more difficult to identify today, although there are more obvious supporting **ammunition storage bunkers** and **personnel shelter bunkers** in the fields here and along La Cache de l'Eglise, which leads away in a different direction from the crossroads. One of the bunkers, found on the track leading to Leoville Rifle Club, later became a Cold War monitoring post for checking radiation levels in the event of a nuclear war.

Leaving behind thoughts of nuclear Armageddon, continue along Rue de la Cour, then turn left onto Rue du Couvent following it until reaching the former St Ouen's Mill. During the Occupation, the Germans added the concrete top to create an **artillery observation post** for Battery Ludendorff. This provided a commanding view over the bay, now becoming visible in front of us, allowing observers to direct artillery fire against Allied ships and invasion forces, using both their guns and others located throughout the island.

Continue past the mill, turning right at the next junction onto Mont Matthieu. Just after the road starts to descend, we reach the first evidence of the German second line of defence in the bay, an **unusual bunker** emblazoned with a title: GESTEINSBOR.KOMP.77. This refers to *Rock Drilling Company 77*, a specialist German unit that built the tunnels behind this bunker linking it to a **command post bunker** in private land on the hill above. Being so proud of their work, the tunnellers presumably decided to leave a permanent reminder of their presence in the island. This bunker, whose machine gun loophole defends the road out of the bay, is part of *Strongpoint Doktorhaus*, which included the command post bunker mentioned and a **heavy** machine gun bunker complete with huge steel turret and a mortar bunker in private land on the other side of the road.

The unusual bunker engraving on Mont Matthieu, denoting the wartime presence of Rock Drilling Company 77

A little way beyond the bunker, the road turns sharply left and the view over St Ouen's Bay opens up dramatically, giving us an opportunity to consider plans for its defence. The seashore is readily visible of course, with some of its many German fortifications evident along with earlier martello towers. Although the intention was for the first line of defence to turn back any invasion on the beach here, a second line of defence was ready to deal with any breakthroughs, holding the attackers in the bay while reinforcements came up to counter-attack. To assist in this, the Germans dug two long anti-tank ditches on either side of St Ouen's Pond that lies below us, and filled the fields behind the beach with mines, barbed wire and anti-tank obstacles. Standing here today, it's hard to imagine the destruction and carnage that would have occurred if this defence in depth had ever been tested.

Continuing down the hill, take Le Chemin Des Hâtiveaux at the next bend and follow it until the junction with Rue de la Val de la Mare, where we turn left. Just after passing into La Route du Moulin, the huge concrete dam of Val de la Mare Reservoir appears on the left while spanning the road ahead is a concrete railway bridge. The Germans built this railway as a means of transport for the vast amount of materials needed to construct the bay's fortifications. To the left of the bridge, the railway's former route is clearly visible running along the valley side towards the dam, while to the right there are the remains of a large earth embankment used to carry the line down into the bay. It is better seen from the next point of interest on our walk.

The Germans created *Resistance Nest La Mare Mill* on the slopes to our left as we look towards the dam, demolishing the water mill that once stood here to ensure a clear field of fire. The principal fortification lies above the small car park, up the sloping path that doglegs round to reach a defile cut into the rock. At its end is the entrance and defensive loophole for a cunningly sited **heavy machine gun bunker** equipped with a huge steel turret, or *sechsschartenturm*, pierced with six loopholes, through which the guns fired. Of the nine of these impressive turrets emplaced in Jersey during the Occupation, only two have survived the post-war scrap drives, one on private ground on Mont Matthieu, and the one here, which we can visit by retracing our steps back from the bunker's entrance and climbing up the small path on the side of the defile. It leads to the top of the bunker where we find the turret complete with granite camouflage. Due to its location, two of the loopholes are blocked, but the remainder continue to dominate the approaches, which during the Second World War would have been cleared of any cover. Two machine guns inside the turret would have been able to keep up a more or less continuous fire, until the bunker fell or the ammunition ran out.

In recent years, the Channel Islands Occupation Society have restored the bunker for opening to the public on occasions. They also cleared some of the shallow trenches and firing positions on the hillside immediately above, while lost in the undergrowth further up the slope are **concrete platforms** for two 7.5cm guns and an **observation bunker**.

After coming back down from the bunker, turn left and follow the path leading to the left hand side of the dam. Here a path cut with steps climbs the valley side to reach the top of the dam, where we turn left to follow the winding gravel track, passing concrete enclosures left over from the dam's construction. Beyond this, the path splits, and we take the left hand route, climbing a little further until the concrete roof of a large bunker appears on the left. This is a telephone exchange bunker, one of several built to house the Germans' complex communications network. A short distance away from its entrance steps is another concrete fortification, this one is an observation and command bunker for the German anti-aircraft battery that once filled this area.

Battery Metz was one of six in the island armed with the much-feared German 8.8cm anti-aircraft gun. There were six guns here during the Occupation, capable of firing at planes up to 10,600 metres above, or supporting the defences of St Ouen's Bay by directly engaging ground targets. When firing at aircraft, a sophisticated targeting system existed, which included a powerful range-finder located in this emplacement that fed height and direction information to a rudimentary computer in the bunker below. It plotted targets, passing aiming details to the guns, which would fire simultaneously to ensure maximum effect. An associated radar installation would assist with tracking targets when line-of-sight was unavailable. With so many of these weapons concentrated in Jersey, it is little wonder Allied planes avoided passing over whenever possible.

From the rear of the command bunker, join the path behind, turning left to follow it until it bends left towards the main road. The emplacements for the 8.8cm guns and shelters for their crews are now lost in the undergrowth to our right and under the gardens of the houses beyond, but here and there it is possible to make out the trenches once connecting the whole battery as they snake across paths and through the undergrowth.

Upon reaching the road, turn right and then left into Rue de la Campagne, which leads us back to Mont Matthieu. Once there, turn right and walk to the church.

The exact age of St Ouen's Church is uncertain, but it dates back a thousand years at least. As the parish church, it housed the cannons of the local Jersey Militia until the 19th century when they moved to purpose-built arsenals. Prior to this, St Ouen's Church was a muster point for the militia, summoned here by the ringing of the church bells. On the morning of 6 January 1781, members of the militia's West Regiment gathered here before marching to St Helier to take part in the Battle of Jersey.

In the churchyard, we find five burials from the First World War, all of which have the distinctive Commonwealth War Graves Commission white headstones. Three have Jersey Militia connections, including **Rifleman Joseph Gionta** who was a member of the 1st (West) Battalion before volunteering for Jersey Contingent, which left the island in March 1915 to join the British Army. They served with the Royal Irish Rifles, which is the badge and regimental name on the headstone, fighting in France and Belgium. Gionta returned to Britain in October 1916, having been wounded or possibly fallen ill while serving at the front, but he appears to have never fully recovered, dying in September 1919 (despite the date on the headstone stating 1920). Elsewhere in the churchyard are the graves of **Sergeant Francis Godfray** and **Private Sydney Ecobichon**, both of whom died while serving with the Royal Jersey Garrison Battalion, a unit created in 1917 to defend the island following the temporary dissolution of the Jersey Militia.

Left: The CWGC headstone of Rifleman Joseph Gionta in St Ouen's Churchyard
Right: Scion of local family, 18-year-old Philip Malet De Carteret before his death in 1916 on HMS Queen Mary

Among the many memorials inside the church, we find another First World War casualty, 18-year-old **Midshipman Philip Malet De Carteret**. The De Carteret family, whose head is Seigneur, or Lord, of the nearby St Ouen's Manor, is one of the oldest and most respected in Jersey. Philip, who was the eldest son of Seigneur Reginald Malet De Carteret, joined the Royal Navy just before the First World War, serving in the South Atlantic and off the Gallipoli Peninsular before sailing with the British battlecruiser HMS *Queen Mary* to face the German fleet in the 1916 Battle of Jutland. HMS *Queen Mary* was one fourteen British ships lost that day, with only eighteen survivors from its crew of 1,266. Philip Malet De Carteret was not among them.

With a final thought for those who lost their lives in war, here at the church ends our walk.

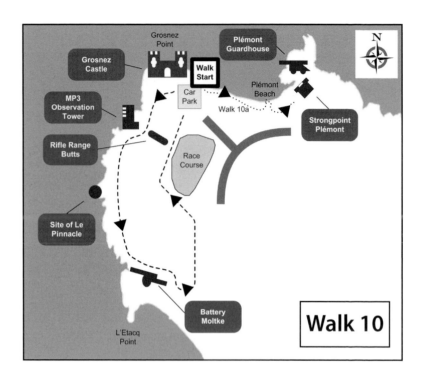

Grosnez Castle gatehouse and towers rise above a man-made ditch unable to prevent the fortification's destruction in the 15th century

Opposite top: MP3 and M2 maintain their lonely vigil over the cliffs of Les Landes

Walk 10: Gatehouse, Guns and Gorse

A ramble around Les Landes from Grosnez Castle to Battery Moltke and back again, with optional walk to the fortifications of Plémont.

There is strong feeling of remoteness associated with Les Landes, which covers Jersey's north-west point. It could be due to the wide-open nature of the gorse-covered headland, or the ruggedness of its towering cliffs and crashing seas. One contributing factor is certainly the area's many derelict and deserted fortifications and military installations, from empty German towers and bunkers to the broken remains of a medieval castle. There is even the long abandoned site of what may be the earliest defended position in Jersey. Yet things have changed at Les Landes recently when it comes to some of the fortifications, as we discover on this easy though at times windswept walk, thanks to some remarkable feats of recovery and restoration.

Start:	Grosnez Castle
Length:	2.5 miles / 2 hours (4 miles / 3 hours with optional walk to Plémont)
Difficulty:	Easy (moderate if optional walk to Plémont is taken)
Getting there –	
By car:	Take the access road from the Route de Grosnez signposted Grosnez Castle and Race Course. Free parking in front of castle
By bus:	Route 8 from Liberation Station, alighting at Grosnez and following the sign to the castle
Refreshments:	None on main walk but café at Plémont (Walk 10a)
Amenities:	None on walk but toilets at Plémont (Walk 10a)

Our walk starts at **Grosnez Castle**, or rather outside its ruined gatehouse. The castle, which was built at the beginning of the 14th century, sits on a narrow promontory thrusting out into the sea towards Sark and Guernsey, which are usually clearly visible from this point. It's a location providing the castle with natural protection on three sides, with only the front susceptible to assault although a man-made ditch, which is still visible today, would have hindered any attackers. The lack of a well within the castle meant that it could not have withstood any prolonged siege, making it more of a stronghold and refuge against raids. Perhaps, as a result, it fell to French invaders at least twice and they may have deliberately destroyed its walls at some point during the 15th century. Today the picturesque remains of its gatehouse and two flanking towers are the most substantial parts of the castle still standing, although a walk around the interior reveals the bases of further walls, towers and buildings.

Walking through the castle, we find beyond evidence of a more modern military installation. A concrete platform marks the site of a **military signal station**. One of a chain of ten such stations set up around Jersey during the Napoleonic Wars to observe shipping and warn of approaching enemies, this particular one communicated with Guernsey, relaying important messages between the islands.

Leaving the castle, take the coastal path towards the distant concrete tower, passing a concrete box-like structure on the left that was once associated with the firing range we visit later on the walk. After a while we arrive at the first German fortification, an **anti-aircraft bunker** with integral crew and ammunitions shelter below. The gun emplacement, which once mounted a 2cm weapon, includes niches for storing ammunition.

Walking a short distance further, we reach what is surely one of the most impressive German fortifications in Jersey, the dramatically situated MP3 (*MP standing for Marinepeilstände und Meßstellen or Naval Coastal Artillery Direction and Range-finding Position*) **naval observation tower**. This is one of three such towers constructed during the Occupation, out of a total of nine originally planned to ring the island. Of the three, this one uniquely had a large radar array installed on top capable of detecting targets over a hundred miles away. Approaching the tower through the defile leading to its base, we pass a large **generator bunker** for powering the radar together with an attached **personnel shelter bunker,** both heavily sealed today. A short distance away is the entrance to the tower, which is also sealed, although for years it stood open to visitors and the elements. Note the **entrance defence loophole,** however, complete with wooden surround added to absorb incoming bullets or shell splinters.

Taking care, those with a head for heights can climb onto the roof of the tower entrance and scan the bottom of the cliffs immediately to the south. Here, at low tide, it's possible to see the **graveyard of heavy artillery guns.** After the Occupation, the returning British forces took measures to demilitarise the island by disposing of all the weapons and ammunition left behind by the Germans. While most of the small guns were dumped far out at sea, 29 of the heaviest were brought here and thrown over the cliffs, where presumably the expectation was they would remain forever. Over the years, however, interest in the rusting weapons grew, leading to an immense effort to haul a number of them back up the cliffs for display purposes, three of which we encounter later on our walk.

Leaving the tower, return to the coastal path and follow it the short distance to more German fortifications, which are another **anti-aircraft bunker** on the left and a split-level **artillery observation bunker** on the right, which is open to carefully inspect. This is M2 (*M standing for Meßstelle or Range-finding Position*), an installation built as an interim measure while the larger MP towers were under construction.

Leaving M2, follow the path along the cliff edge once more, noting the fine views of **Le Pinnacle** in front, a huge natural rock formation standing proud of the cliff face. Near its base are some of the earliest evidence of human settlement in Jersey, including possible **defensive ramparts** dating back to the Neolithic and Bronze Ages, together with the remains of what appears to be a Roman temple. It is possible to visit this site, although care must be taken on the path down. Continue over the shallow valley via the narrow wooden footbridge and, after passing a number of half-buried shooting pits,we arrive at a large and partially overgrown concrete platform. This is the first trace of an extensive German installation once located here at Les Landes.

Viewed from a German anti-aircraft gun emplacement, Le Pinnacle is possibly the site of the oldest fortifications in Jersey

Battery Moltke was a heavy coastal artillery unit armed with four 15.5cm guns capable of hitting targets over twelve miles away. These weapons, which dated back to the First World War, were captured from the French Army after the fall of France in June 1940, and

The presence of an original ex-French 15.5cm heavy gun helps make the restored No. 1 emplacement of Battery Moltke one of the finest in Europe today

sent to Jersey as an interim measure pending the arrival of more modern naval guns from Germany. As a result, each gun position had two concrete emplacements built, one for the French guns, one for the German. Allied bombing of Germany meant the latter never arrived and so the older guns remained in place for the rest of the war. Here at **Gun Position No. 4** the overgrown nature of the site means this arrangement is not obvious, nor at **Gun Position No. 3** that we reach by following the coastal path noting two small **bunkers for tank turrets** further inland to protect the battery from land-based attack.

A little further on and we arrive at **Gun Position No. 2,** and here the emplacement for the French 15.5cm gun is largely clear of vegetation. It contains the remarkable remains of a **gun barrel,** although not one from Battery Moltke or from the bottom of the cliffs. The **shattered steel parts come from a 22cm gun** once emplaced at Battery Roon near Beauport Bay. In August 1944, while firing at British naval vessels off Jersey's south coast a shell exploded inside the barrel. Years later, the buried remains of that barrel were found under the earth of the prison garden now located in that area, and transported here. Looking at them today, spare a thought for the poor gun crew on that fateful night, one of whom was killed while a number of others were wounded.

Walking on, continue along the cliff path passing a small **one man bunker** overlooking the cliff-edge and another split-level **artillery observation bunker**, this one designated M2a, which may have been used as the Battery Moltke command and fire-control post. A short distance further and we arrive at **Gun Position No. 1,** today in the care of the Channel Islands Occupation Society, which has done a remarkable job of restoration and recovery here to present one of the best preserved Second World War fortifications in Europe.

The work undertaken here, and the presence of an original gun, allows us to understand the emplacements of Battery Moltke fully. The one in which the 15.5cm gun currently resides is the 'temporary' emplacement, while the one for the 'modern' gun sits alongside and today contains two **other recovered barrels**. Also visible in niches around this latter emplacement are three **metal ammunition hoists** connecting it to concealed **ammunition storage bunkers** located behind and linked by concrete tunnels. A tunnel also links the emplacements to a **personnel shelter bunker** for the gun crew, located still further back near the car park and today the access point for the complex when it is open to the public. When it became obvious the modern guns would not arrive, the 'temporary' emplacement was linked to the ammunition and personnel bunkers via a ramp, which can be seen just behind. On clearing this ramp during the restoration, the concrete sentry box seen nearby was found having presumably been dumped as backfill after the Occupation. Note its inscribed date of 20 10 42, presumably added at the time of construction.

Leaving the gun emplacements, take the road that leads inland, passing a number of metal anti-tank obstacles that once stood on Jersey's beaches or in the coastal area behind. Also partially visible on either side among the undergrowth are anti-aircraft bunkers once armed with 3.7cm anti-aircraft guns to protect against attacks on the battery by low-flying aircraft. Passing them, we eventually arrive at a low metal gate on the left, from where two paths lead off. Take the left hand one marked footpath and follow it, passing a model aircraft strip on the left before reaching a gravel road that leads us further back towards Grosnez Castle. Just past a small car park, the path forks – take the route on the left keeping the racecourse on the right-hand side. Ahead, the butts and target holders of the shooting range are visible, while hidden in the undergrowth on the left are several lines of shooting pits. Stop on reaching the butts.

The rifle range was first used by the Jersey Rifle Association after it was formed in 1861 for the purpose of 'encouraging competition in the use of the rifle'. Consisting mostly of members of the Jersey Militia, the value of good marksmanship was recognised by the Association, which organised 'Prize Meetings' here for many years. During the Occupation, the Germans used and extensively damaged the range, although shooting returned after the war.

Passing the rifle butts, follow the path back to Grosnez Castle and our starting point.

Enigmatic German machine gun emplacement at Plemont, built on top of a far earlier fortification

Walk 10a: Visit to the Fortifications of Plémont

From the car park by Grosnez Castle, a sign points to the well-established cliff path leading away east along Jersey's north coast. The route winds around the rugged heights of this quiet part of the island, before dropping down into the narrow valley leading to Plémont Bay.

Plémont boasts one of Jersey's most beautiful beaches, although the fact it is covered at high tide renders it a more selective choice for all except adventurous surfers who gather here regardless to wait for the perfect wave. On reaching the road leading to the bay, turn left to follow it down to the café situated high above the beach. At the top of the steps descending to the café, we find another **precast concrete German sentry box**, again with an inscribed date of 14 10 42. There were guards here in the First World War as well, when men from the Jersey Militia's 1st (West) Battalion took turns to watch over the telegraph cables that landed here and terminated in the building that is used today as public toilets. Prior to 1914, there was only a single cable coming ashore here that connected Jersey to the UK via Guernsey. After the outbreak of war, however, the British cut a formerly German undersea cable running through the Channel and diverted it to provide a direct connection for military traffic between Jersey and England.

Behind the concrete sentry box, a path cut with steps take us to an upper car park. The land beyond was once the location for the Plémont Holiday Camp, which stood derelict and under threat of development for many years. In 2015, having acquired the site, the National Trust for Jersey finally demolished the former camp and restored the land to a natural state. Clearing the buildings revealed a number of German fortifications, elements of Stongpoint Plémont, constructed to protect this part of the coast. Cut across the car park to reach a tarmac road which we follow east until the cliff path leads away to the left once more. From the small car park here, a path leads to a German split-level **artillery observation bunker**, designated M3, for many years engulfed by the camp. Located nearby are other bunkers, mortar positions and shelters.

A little way along the cliff path we find an enigmatic little **granite turret emplacement,** actually built by the Germans on top of a former **guardhouse dating to the 18th century** for the mounting of two machine guns (see illustration page 105). Below this position, further granite and concrete fortifications are visible, with a narrow path winding down to them. The granite parts of this site are from a small 19th century fort equipped with a light cannon and a powder magazine for its ammunition. The concrete parts are additions from the Occupation of course, with a **bunker for tank turret** once armed with a machine gun and a **searchlight shelter bunker** for a 60cm searchlight that would have emerged from either end to illuminate targets at night time.

After exploring the fortifications here, we can return to the walk's start at Grosnez Castle either by taking the cliff path or by walking inland from Plémont and turning right to follow the Route Des Grantez. A pleasant optional alternative is to stop at the excellent Plémont Café for refreshments before the walk back.

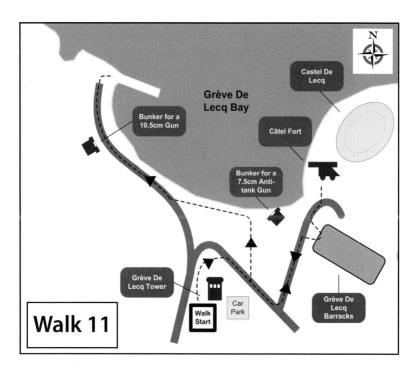

Map labels:
- **Grève De Lecq Bay**
- Castel De Lecq
- Bunker for a 10.5cm Gun
- Câtel Fort
- Bunker for a 7.5cm Anti-tank Gun
- Grève De Lecq Tower
- Walk Start
- Car Park
- Grève De Lecq Barracks

Walk 11

*Castel de Lecq, a three thousand year old fortification still
towering above the golden sands of Grève de Lecq*

Walk 11: The Soldier's Bay

A short stroll around Grève de Lecq's three thousand years of fortifications and defences.

The little bay of Grève de Lecq on the north-west coast is one of the island's most popular, especially when the sun is shining down on its distinctive golden sands. The modern day welcome found here contrasts with its distinctly military past, however, which saw the bay fortified from the Iron Age to the end of the Second World War. On this short, but very rewarding walk, we visit what remains of those fortifications as well as passing by plenty of locations for a well-deserved ice cream or refreshing drink.

Start:	Car park in the centre of the bay
Length:	1 mile / 1 hour
Difficulty:	Easy, but with one steep hill to climb and descend
Getting there –	
By car:	Free parking around the tower in the centre of the bay, although in the summer it can become full.
By bus:	Route 9 from Liberation Station, alighting at Grève de Lecq
Refreshments:	A good choice of restaurants, bars and cafés in and around the bay
Amenities:	Public toilets above beach

Within the car park we find our first fortification, a **Conway-style round** tower built towards the end of the 1770s on the orders of the then lieutenant governor, General Henry Conway. It was probably one of the first constructed in the island, with the bay's relative closeness to France perhaps being the motivation. Although located some way back from the beach, its single 18-pounder cannon emplaced on top was able to fire on any invaders entering the bay, while the tower itself could protect the two routes leading inland from here.

During the Occupation, the Germans incorporated the tower into their *Strongpoint Grève De Lecq*, the group of fortifications responsible for defending the bay, reinforcing its entrance and the interior and placing twin machine guns on top. There was also a mortar position at the top of the car park and another behind the Prince of Wales Hotel opposite, which was used as a billet by the Germans stationed here.

Leave the tower and walk through the car park towards the sea. On the right-hand side at its bottom are a small set of steps down to the road. Take these and after a short walk along the pavement, cross the road to climb a little way up Le Chemin du Câtel and reach the entrance to the barracks.

We have arrived at **Grève de Lecq Barracks**, built in 1810 at the height of the Napoleonic Wars, along with several others in the island. Today, they are the only examples that remain in a recognisable condition thanks to the efforts of the National Trust for Jersey which acquired them in 1972. The buildings we see are a mix of dormitories for the officers and men, washrooms, storerooms and stables. At the back is a small cell block with two rooms for any wrongdoers. They would have accommodated up to 250 soldiers, although the squeeze for such a number can be appreciated. Mostly the occupants were regular army soldiers, part of the British Army garrison stationed in the island until the early 1930s, although at other times they were used by the Jersey Militia, notably during the First World War. The barracks are usually open to the public between May and September on certain days of the week, with details on dates and times available on the National Trust for Jersey's website.

Leaving the barracks continue up the steep Le Chemin du Câtel, which bends sharply after a short distance. Just beyond this, we find a track leading to Câtel Fort on the left, which, subject to there being no warnings that shooting is taking place at the Crabbé Firing Ranges further up the hill, we follow until reaching the fort.

Along with two other cannon batteries on the opposite side of the bay and the round tower in the centre, the powerful little **Câtel Fort** defended Grève de Lecq during the Napoleonic Wars. Initially just a platform for three 32-pounder cannon, a guardhouse for fifteen soldiers was later added, along with a magazine, defensive walls and a small entrance defence position visible today to the right of the gate against the earth bank. Like the barracks below, Câtel Fort is owned today by the National Trust and, although not normally open, can be hired by the public.

The hill on which the fort stands, and which now towers above us, contains a far older fortification that still dominates Grève de Lecq, but we shall consider it from a distance later in the walk, when its features are more readily visible. Leaving the fort, we retrace our steps to the road and descend past the barracks until reaching the main road. Turn right and after passing the millennium cross, turn right again to walk through the car park of Café Romany and its outside seating area to arrive on the walkway above the beach.

Immediately to our right, there is a German **bunker for a 7.5cm anti-tank gun**, with its fearsome former weapon capable of firing

A bunker for a 7.5cm anti-tank gun sits quietly on one side of Grève de Lecq today

a high explosive shell up to four and half miles. In Jersey, there were only four emplaced in bunkers like this one, so it is something of a rarity. Tucked menacingly into this corner of the bay and protected by the mass of the cliff to its right, it would have presented a formidable challenge to any force attempting the land here.

Leaving the bunker, follow the path and road around the top of the beach, passing another popular café after which we arrive at a German **bunker for a 10.5cm gun**, with its weapon capable of firing at targets

Grève de Lecq's bunker for a 10.5cm gun as it appeared during the Occupation
(CIOS Collection)

up to just over seven miles away. Walk on towards the pier, built in 1872 but 13 years later partially destroyed in a storm leaving the remains seen at low tide stretching out from the end. On the left, the small untidy building behind the granite wall is a **searchlight shelter bunker** that once housed a 60cm searchlight, used by Grève de Lecq's German defenders to illuminate any attackers approaching the bay under cover of darkness. On the pier itself, there is a small **bunker for a tank turret** once armed with a small anti-tank gun and machine gun.

While here, it is a good place to consider the hill above the opposite side of the bay, which is potentially the remains of one of the earliest fortifications found today in Jersey. The **Castel de Lecq** is an 81-metre high mound with clear traces of ancient and apparently man-made banks and ditches, leading to the conclusion it was once an Iron Age promontory fort, dating back more than three thousand years. As such, it was probably built to both defend the safe anchorage here, and provide a place of refuge for the local inhabitants should the island come under attack. In the latter role, it may have remained in use until the Middle Ages, alongside Mont Orgueil Castle, Grosnez Castle and other earthwork structures. The passing of time means we may never know the mound's precise nature and use, but the enigmatic sight of it rising above the bay provides a fitting end to our walk.

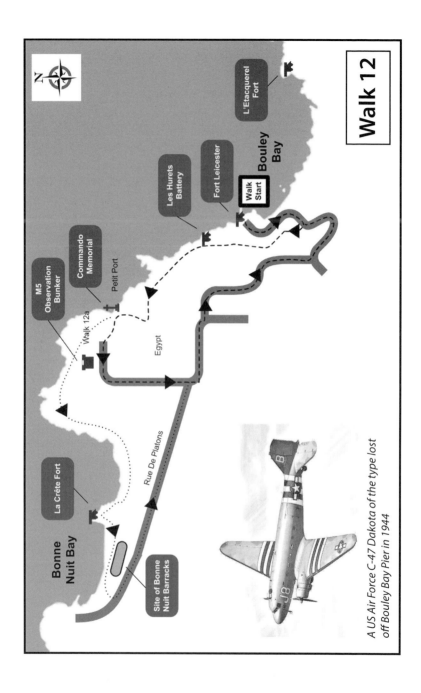

Walk 12

N

L'Etacquerel Fort

Les Hurets Battery

Fort Leicester

Walk Start

Bouley Bay

Commando Memorial

M5 Observation Bunker

Petit Port

Walk 12a

Egypt

La Crête Fort

Bonne Nuit Bay

Rue De Platons

Site of Bonne Nuit Barracks

A US Air Force C-47 Dakota of the type lost off Bouley Bay Pier in 1944

Walk 12: Russians and Raiders

An energetic trek from Bouley Bay to Petit Port and back with optional extended walk to La Crête Fort at Bonne Nuit.

While the towering cliffs of Jersey's north coast may form a natural bulwark against attack, the many small bays and coves found here have always been weaknesses in the armour and fortified through the centuries as a result. On this walk, we visit some of these defences, from forts to bunkers, all set among some of Jersey's most rugged but beautiful coastal scenery, and consider some of the men stationed here in past times, from local militia to renegade Russians. We also retrace the steps of the only British Commando raid on Jersey during the Second World War, a courageous but ultimately tragic attempt to discover the truth about the German Occupation.

Starting point:	Bouley Bay Pier
Length:	3.5 miles / 2.5 hours, increasing to 6.5 miles / 4 hours with an extension to Bonne Nuit
Difficulty:	Challenging, with steep cliff paths to climb and descend
Getting there –	
By car:	Free parking on the pier and road leading down to Bouley Bay
By bus:	None in winter, but Route 4 calls in six times daily on its return journey from Bonne Nuit on summer weekdays
Refreshments:	Café at Bouley Bay
Amenities:	Public toilets at Bouley Bay

Given its reputation as a centre for scuba diving, it seems appropriate to consider the waters off Bouley Bay before turning our attention to its land-based military history. Several wrecks lie under the waters near the pier we are now standing on, mostly due to accidents or deliberate sinking. There is one, however, dating to the Second World War, which is the sunken reminder of a tragic event that happened here towards the end of the Occupation.

In October 1944, a **US Air Force C-47 Dakota** lost its way while flying from Paris to Cherbourg and, uncertain of his position, the pilot turned on his landing lights to indicate he was in trouble. Unfortunately, the plane was over hostile Jersey at the time, and a German anti-aircraft battery located above Bouley Bay ignored the distress signal and opened fire hitting the Dakota, which made a forced landing in the seas off the pier. The survivors swam towards the shore, but found the heavy swell prevented a landing while strong waves dashed them against the rocks at the foot of the nearby cliffs. One by one, all drowned until only the pilot, Lieutenant Bob Backler, remained alive. Eventually German rescuers arrived with a rope and managed to haul him to safety. Lieutenant Backler spent the rest of the war in the POW camp at Mount Bingham while the bodies of his comrades were buried in the military cemetery found in Howard Davis Park (both visited on Walk 17). The Dakota, less its propellers, which have been recovered and put on display at the Jersey War Tunnels, remains under the water off Bouley Bay Pier, a sad testament to that tragic night.

Turning our attention back onshore, above the pier is a granite fortification with concrete additions here and there. This is **Fort Leicester**, which was built in 1836 on the site of earlier fortifications dating back more than two centuries. There was a battery of cannons first placed here to defend the anchorage following a French attack in 1549, and named after the Earl of Leicester, a favourite of Queen Elizabeth. By the time of the Napoleonic Wars two hundred years later, it had become a small fort, defending the bay alongside three other cannon batteries, although most were dismantled after Napoleon's final defeat in 1815. Renewed tensions between Britain and France in the 1830s, however, led to the construction of Fort Leicester as we see it today, armed with five 32-pounder cannon to defend the bay along with **L'Etaquerel Fort** visible across the waters of the bay (visited on Walk 13). During the Occupation, the Germans modified its defences to include a **searchlight shelter bunker** and a **machine gun emplacement**.

Leave the pier and walk inland, passing the slipway on our left before reaching the public toilets just beyond where there are more remains of the German defences, which were collectively designed *Resistance Nest Bouley Hafen*. On top of the low granite wall next to the public toilets, note the swastika carved into the stone, while beyond the toilets and on the other side of a **garage-type bunker** that once housed a 10.5cm gun, a further inscription showing another **swastika and the date 1943** is just visible on a patch of concrete. Clearly the soldiers here felt the need to record their presence for posterity.

Leaving the bay behind, begin to walk up the road until reaching the start of the cliff path to Bonne Nuit on our right. Before taking it, however, cross the road to inspect the walls of the property opposite on which we find the inscription 1944 POA carved into the brickwork, and left here by the Russian soldiers once guarding this part of the island.

After their invasion of the Soviet Union in 1941, the Germans took a huge number of prisoners-of-war, some of whom later volunteered to serve in the German Army. Their motives for doing so were many, including an understandable desire to escape the terrible German treatment of Soviet prisoners. In 1943, a battalion of these volunteers arrived in Jersey and were allocated a role defending the island's north coast. Identifiable by an arm badge bearing the letters POA, which is a Cyrillic letters abbreviation for **Russian Liberation Army**, although locals took the badge to mean 'Pals of Adolf'. What they made of their

The shoulder badge of the Russian Liberation Army volunteers, or 'Pals of Adolf' as the locals called them

lonely posting here in Jersey is impossible to say as few would survive the aftermath of the Second World War to tell their story. Understandably regarded as traitors, after being handed back to Russia in 1945, most were either executed or sent to work in Siberian labour camps for the remainder of their lives. This little inscription is all that remains to remind us of their presence here in Jersey.

Returning to the cliff path, follow it steeply up out of the bay stopping to draw breath and admire the increasingly spectacular views. After reaching the top, the path follows a grassy track before a signpost points to the coastal path climbing once more to the right before flattening out upon reaching the top of the hill. After passing some trees alongside the path, depending on the height of undergrowth it may be possible to see a small ruined structure higher up on the right-hand side. This guardhouse and magazine was once part of **Les Hurets Battery**, which during the Napoleonic Wars had two 12-pounder cannons situated on a platform a little way in front. Due to the undergrowth here, it can be difficult to approach the guardhouse today, but any views from the cliff edge show the wonderful field of fire it once enjoyed.

Continue along the cliff path as it winds up and down the contours, offering many magnificent views along the coast or across the seas past offshore reefs to France. In due course, a wooded valley cuts across our path, and, as we turn inland to follow its side, there is a glimpse of a small granite building far below situated above a small cove known as Petit Port. This is our next point of interest. Follow the path down the steep side of the valley to a stream at the bottom where we turn right taking the wide path signposted Bonne Nuit. Eventually we arrive at the granite hut and a small stone memorial recalling a courageous but ultimately tragic event that took place on Christmas Day night in 1943.

Operation Hardtack 28 was the code name for a British Commando raid that landed at Petit Port to investigate the German defences and try to learn how the island was coping with occupation. Led by 22-year-old Captain Philip Ayton, the raiding party of nine British and French commandos came ashore by a small boat after crossing the Channel in a Royal Navy warship. Discovering this small hut, which is a former guardhouse probably used at the time solely by fishermen, was empty, they set off up the valley via the path we have just walked down. They were fortunate because, as they discovered, their route had taken them straight through a minefield. Leaving this

The memorial to the British Commandos at Petit Port

behind, the party climbed the right-hand side of the valley and discovered an empty German artillery observation bunker. Pushing further inland, they visited two farms, learning from the occupants of one that the Germans (or actually Russians) had a strongpoint some distance away. With time running out, they approached this but finding it surrounded by barbed wire and mines, decided to return to Petit Port and their boat. On arrival, they realised their boat was missing, and set off along the path towards Bonne Nuit in search of it, unknowingly entering another minefield. Here their luck ran out, and Captain Ayton was badly wounded after stepping on a mine. The commotion did at least alert the Royal Navy vessel offshore, which sent a boat to pick them up. Captain Ayton survived the journey back to the UK, but died of his injuries the next day.

Today, the memorial we see commemorates the Commando raid and Captain Ayton's death. In recent years, there has been a short but moving ceremony conducted here to remember the men who landed that night in 1943, with bugler and wreaths to recall their bravery and sacrifice. Depending on the time of year we visit, the signs of the ceremony may be present. Also present is a **memorial bench donated by the Special Boat Service, or SBS**, the modern day descendant of the Second World War's seaborne raiders.

The next part of our walk traces, as practically as possible, the route taken by the Operation Hardtack Commandos, before leading us back to Bouley Bay. As an alternative, however, you may prefer to follow **Walk 12a**, which continues on the cliff path to visit La Crête Fort at Bonne Nuit, the details of which are at the end of this chapter.

To continue this walk, we must retrace our steps up the valley.

119

After arriving back at the place we descended into the valley, turn right over the stream to follow the path, which climbs up past some ruined buildings. The wartime commandos continued further up the valley before turning right through a small abandoned village called Egypt that the Germans had commandeered for training purposes. Eventually our dirt track becomes a tarmac road, at which point we are roughly back on the Commandos' path once more. Continue along this road for around two hundred metres, when it bends sharply to the left, and a farm track leads off to the right. The German split-level **artillery observation bunker**, designated M5 (*M standing for Meßstelle or Range-finding Position*) that the Commandos visited that night is up this track and in a field to the right. After the Occupation, it was one of a handful of bunkers retained by the island's authorities and used for civil defence purposes. If you want to visit the bunker, remember that these are private agricultural fields and should be respected as such.

Back at the road bend, note the '**spang marks**' on the wall made from bullets or shrapnel – could they date from the time when the Germans used this as a battle training ground, or are they more recent? Follow the road inland, once again tracing the steps of the Commandos. To the right, on the high ground near the houses, are the remains of the German strongpoint visited that night, but not entered. Eventually, this road, La Rue d'Égypte, arrives at a main road (which is also where Walk 12a rejoins) where we should stop.

Directly ahead is a house called **La Geonnière**, which in 1943 was a farm, inhabited by a Miss Le Feuvre who on hearing the Commandos knocking on her door sent them away, thinking they were a German patrol. The second farm they visited, belonging to **John and Hedley Le Breton** is among the buildings below us on the left and now mostly concealed by the greenery. Here the Commandos had more luck, with the Le Breton brothers offering a glass of milk and revealing all they knew about the German occupation. The Le Bretons, who were honoured after the war by the French for the help provided, also directed the Commandos towards the nearby German strongpoint, which today is near the large aerial masts we can see. Here we leave the Commandos, but spare a final thought for those brave men on Christmas night 1943. For young Captain Ayton at least, it was to be his last.

Follow the main road past La Geonnière which winds along until we reach a sharp bend to the right at which point a small road called La Vielle Charrière leads straight ahead. Take this to descend steeply down into Bouley Bay, noting on the left a fine view of **Les Hurets Guardhouse** sitting on the high ground above the cliffs. Eventually, this small road reaches the main one winding down to the bay, and it was near here that a bloody battle was fought in 1549 when the local soldiers of the Jersey Militia faced a powerful force that had landed in Bouley Bay intent on invading the island.

The French King Henry II, sent a force under Captain François Breuil to attack the Channel Islands in 1549, and they **landed here in Bouley Bay** hoping for an easy victory. But assembled on these slopes were the men of the Jersey Militia, mustered to defend their homes and their island. On that day, they did just that, bravely holding their ground to defeat Breuil and his men, forcing the survivors to hastily re-embark and flee back to France. The French King was so dismayed at the defeat that he forbade any mention of it.

With a thought to the steadfastness of Jerseymen on that day, follow the road down the hill and to the pier for a return to the start of our walk.

Members of the 2nd (East) Battalion of the Jersey Militia at Bonne Nuit Barracks during the First World War

Walk 12a: To La Crête Fort and Bonne Nuit

Leaving the Commando memorial at Petit Port, continue along the coastal path, recalling that within the first fifty metres or so is the place where Captain Ayton would have encountered the deadly minefield. The path skirts some magnificent cliff-edge scenery, climbing steeply at times, with the reward of magnificent vistas upon reaching the top. Above a rocky cove called Giffard Bay, the path splits, with our route the lower track to the right. After travelling around the bay, we eventually arrive at a granite fortification that has been visible in the distance – the handsome **La Crête Fort**.

There appears to have been a fortified position at or near this location since the 16th century, perhaps a cannon battery with earthwork defences. By the time of the Napoleonic Wars, a guardhouse had been added here, and another battery existed higher up the headland. In 1834, in response to the renewed threat from France, this fort was constructed and armed with six cannon, together with a magazine and accommodation for one officer and thirty men. As the threat from France receded, so too did the need for the fort, that is until the Germans arrived in 1940 and modified it to create *Resistance Nest Bonne Nuit Fort*, complete with concrete bunkers and emplacements for machine guns, an anti-tank gun and searchlight. In addition, they created a **detached fortification for a small anti-tank gun**, visible today close to the waterline facing Bonne Nuit Bay, while on the rocky outcrop opposite the fort's gate is an **emplacement for an 8.2cm mortar**, clad in camouflaging granite.

After the Occupation, the dry ditch that protected the entrance was filled in with the accommodation we can see today, and it became the holiday home of the island's lieutenant governor for a time. Today, it is a Jersey Heritage holiday let, and so the interior cannot be visited without permission.

Leaving the fort, take the gravel roadway leading away towards Bonne Nuit Bay, which can be seen clearly from here. Soon we arrive at an area of buildings, today a hotel and homes, but until the 1930s the site of **Bonne Nuit Barracks**, built during the Napoleonic Wars to help accommodate the growing number of soldiers on the island. They remained in use until the First World War, but in the years that followed they became a hotel until finally demolished in the 1950s. Today little remains although a small square stone on the left-hand side as we pass through, bears the inscription **W↑D** to indicate a War Department marker stone denoting the area's former owners.

The main road down to Bonne Nuit is soon reached. Our walk goes left up the hill, but you may want to visit the pretty harbour of Bonne Nuit, with its excellent café, by turning right.

Continue up the road, called Les Nouvelles Charrières, until the top. Bearing left, the road flattens out and we follow it, passing a gravel car park on the left in which a popular little mobile café is usually in residence. Keep on walking along this road, Les Rue Des Platons, passing various communication masts and electronic installations. Just before reaching the junction with La Rue d'Égypte, where we re-join the main Walk 12 to return to Bouley Bay, note that in the fields to our left was once an extensive **Jersey Militia firing range**, with some remains of ammunition stores found among the houses here.

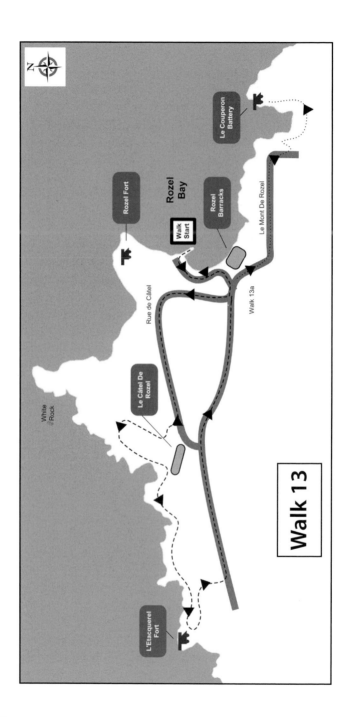

Walk 13

Walk 13: Picture Perfect

A circular walk from Rozel past Le Câtel de Rozel going west towards Bouley Bay, with optional walk east to visit Le Couperon Battery. When it comes to picture perfect, Rozel Bay and Harbour must come close to having it all, with the verdant green backdrop, sheltered little beach, charming coloured huts and a good selection of restaurants, bars and cafés. Yet like all of Jersey's other north coast bays, the sheltered waters of Rozel offered a landing place for would-be invaders and needed defending as a result. On this circular walk, we see evidence of these defences, including some of the earliest purpose-built fortifications in the island.

Start:	Rozel Pier
Length:	2.5 miles / 2 hours, extending to 4 miles / 3.5 hours with a visit to Le Couperon Battery
Difficulty:	Moderate: some steep climbs and descents both on roads and paths
Getting there –	
By car:	Free parking at Rozel although it will quickly fill up in the summer.
By bus:	Route 3 from Liberation Station, alighting at Rozel
Refreshments:	A choice of cafés, bars and restaurants at Rozel
Amenities:	Public toilets on Rozel Pier

Rozel Bay has offered a sheltered anchorage and landing place long before the completion in 1832 of the pier we are now standing on. This fact, and its close proximity to the French coast, clearly visible from here on most days, marked it out as a potential place for enemy attack, which in turn led to defensive precautions dating back to at least the 17th century. By the start of the 19th century, during the heightened threat caused by the Napoleonic Wars, these defences had expanded to include several batteries of cannon on both sides and in the centre of the bay, and an important new fortification visible today among the buildings above the beach.

Rozel or **Le Couperon Barracks** were completed here in 1810, built on the orders of General Don, then the island's lieutenant-governor, as one of three new barracks constructed in bays along the north coast, the others being at Grève de Lecq and Bonne Nuit. The outer walls of Rozel barracks remain today complete with defensive musket loopholes, although their interior has long since given way to modern development.

In addition to the defences in the bay, two large 24-pounder cannon were mounted in a battery located on the Nez de Guet Headland, in fortifications that later became **Rozel Fort**, today a grand property sitting on the hill above the pier. During the Occupation, the Germans took over Rozel Fort, re-arming it with machine guns, a mortar, flamethrowers, a 10.5cm artillery gun and several searchlights. There was also a 3.7cm anti-tank gun located in an emplacement

Unusual structure that once protected an anti-tank gun below Rozel Fort

with the distinctive **concrete cover** clearly visible situated below the fort closer to the waterline. These defences were designated *Resistance Nest Rozel Fort*, while those here on the pier, consisting of **bunkers for** tank turrets armed with a machine gun and a 3.7cm anti-tank gun, were called *Resistance Nest Rozel Hafen*. One of these turrets was at the end of the pier, while the other was located near its base.

Walking back along the pier and round the edge of the harbour, take the road out of the bay until it reaches the junction with the main road. At this point, we take a sharp right to climb the small and initially steep little road called Rue du Câtel, which offers stunning views over the bay as it rises. After winding past the entrances of a number of prestigious properties, including that of Rozel Fort, the road flattens and straightens out with fields on our right and views over Rozel Valley and Woods to the left. After a while, the road turn left, and here we find a track going right indicated by a sign marked 'Footpath' that we follow. Within a short distance, a large earth bank rises up to our left.

The bank is of course man-made, the dramatic remnants of a huge earthen fortification once located here called **Le Câtel de Rozel**. Although little is known today about the site, it was almost certainly an Iron Age promontory fort, protected naturally on three sides by cliffs and along its other by this earthen rampart, which would have been considerably longer in ancient times. Archaeological evidence suggests it remained in use through the Roman period, and may have continued to offer protection against invaders into the Middle Ages. Pause for a moment to consider the work put in three thousand years ago by the island's inhabitants at the time, labouring by hand to construct their defences here. They clearly felt threatened by a terrible enemy to go to such efforts.

The great earthen rampart, all that remains of the Iron Age Le Câtel de Rozel.

Walking on, follow the track first away from the earthen bank, then sharp left into a small public car park from where intrepid anglers venture down to the highly-regarded fishing mark called 'White Rock' away to the right. Our route takes us straight through the car park, however, past the wooden gate to reach the start of the coastal path proper, again sign-posted 'Footpath'. This part of the cliff path is one of the easier sections, although there are one or two moderate climbs and descents, so take time to enjoy the views back towards White Rock and forward towards Bouley Bay, identifiable in the distance by its short pier. It can get muddy and somewhat slippery following wet weather here, so take care if this is the case. In due course, a wooden stile gate appears across our route, straight after which another path joins from the left. We will take this latter path shortly, but first carry on along the cliff path for a short distance until it splits again, taking the route descending down to the right. Ahead looms the granite walls of a small fortification.

L'Etaquerel Fort was built in 1835/36 to defend Bouley Bay at a time of renewed tensions between Britain and France. There was a defensive position mounting cannon in this location prior to this, with origins perhaps dating back to the 16th century, but situated higher up than the present fort, and certainly less elaborate. Today Jersey Heritage manages L'Etaquerel Fort as a holiday let, and so it is not generally open to the public, but from the outside, it is possible to get an impression of the design and scale. The fort was defended on the landward side by the dry ditch we see in front of the walls, which are loop-holed to allow musket fire on anyone approaching. Inside are four emplacements for 32-pounder cannons, which would have been mounted on fixed carriages that permitted a limited traverse but that fully covered the approaches to the bay in front. There is accommodation for the garrison of one officer and forty men, and a magazine capable of storing up to ninety barrels of gunpowder. All in all, a splendid little fort.

Leaving the fort, climb back up the path and return to the wooden stile gate, taking the path to the right, which climbs to reach a small car park. The main road is just a short distance from here, where we turn left and follow it back down to Rozel Bay, enjoying the valley views on the right and noting Le Câtel de Rozel towering above on the left. Our walk finishes upon reaching Rozel Bay again, although those still with energy can follow Walk 13a to visit the well preserved Napoleonic Wars era Le Couperon Battery.

*The loop-holed walls of L'Etaquerel Fort above
the dry ditch dug to defend its landward side*

Walk 13a: Le Couperon Battery

Rather than taking the route down to the beach and pier, continue along the main road through Rozel, passing the Rozel Bay pub on the right and a second road down to the beach on the left before leaving the bay on Le Mont de Rozel. The road climbs gradually, offering great views over the bay and harbour once more. Eventually we reach a sharp bend to the right, shortly after which there is a track leading off to the left opposite a bus stop and signposted 'Public footpath to Le Scez'. Taking this, we plunge down into a small wooded valley with a gloomy little pond at the bottom, before climbing out again on the other side. Eventually, the path opens as a field above the small car park above Saie Harbour is reached. Crossing the top of the field, we arrive at the Dolmen du Couperon, a Neolithic gallery grave dating back more than four thousand years, behind which is a small two-door building.

This is the magazine and guardhouse for **Le Couperon Battery**, originally constructed at the end of the 17th century, but remodelled in the years that followed. By the time of the Napoleonic Wars, the battery mounted two 24-pounder cannon on an open platform behind the building. From here, it's possible to appreciate the field of fire for these guns, which had a range of around one mile allowing them to sweep not only Rozel Bay ahead, but also command its seaward approaches. The troops manning the battery would have been members of the Jersey Militia, men from the local 2nd or North Regiment most likely, coming down here from the surrounding farms to take up station in times of alarm or simply when on guard duty. Perhaps it wasn't too onerous a duty, particularly on a fine day or evening, but then they would have known that just a short distance across the water was France, in those days a sworn enemy.

With the walk complete, we can retrace our steps to Rozel, or if you came by bus, there are stops back on Le Mont De Rozel.

*Rozel Barracks, built in 1810 but changed considerably
since by modern day development*

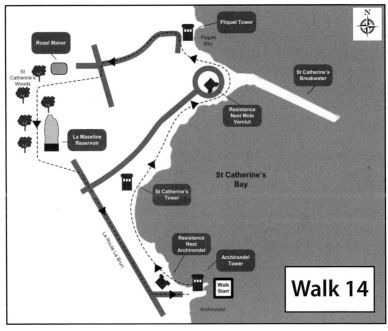

Archirondel Tower, built in 1794 and heavily modified during the Occupation

Walk 14: Enemy Over the Water

From Archirondel to Fliquet and back, taking in St Catherine's Bay, Breakwater and Woods.

St Catherine's Bay contains one of Jersey's most enigmatic sights – a massive breakwater stretching out to sea with little apparent purpose other than for anglers and the shelter of a few small boats. Yet the nearby coast of France holds a clue to its true purpose, as does the stump of massive blocks found at Archirondel, where our walk starts and ends. The half-complete harbour here is a reminder of an enemy over the water, as are the intriguing range of fortifications and sites of military interest encountered on this very pleasant coastal and inland walk.

Start:	Archirondel Tower
Length:	4 miles / 3 hours
Difficulty:	Moderate, with a few climbs and descents, sometimes on paths that are slippery in wet weather.
Getting there –	
By car:	Free parking at Archirondel although it will quickly fill up in the summer.
By bus:	Route 2 to St Catherine (summer only), alighting at Archirondel.
Refreshments:	Cafés at Archirondel and St Catherine's breakwater
Amenities:	Public toilets at Archirondel and St Catherine's breakwater

Having arrived at Archirondel, make your way to the prominently marked tower where our walk begins. This **Conway-style round tower** was one of the last of this type built in Jersey, and differed from all others except La Rocco Tower in St Ouen's Bay by the inclusion of a masonry platform around its base. Unlike La Rocco Tower, however, or any of the others in the island, note that this one has only three, rather than four, of the distinctive protruding 'machiolations' around the top – although the reason why is unclear. Completed in 1794 at a cost of £4,000, it mounted four 18-pounder cannon, three in fixed emplacements at the bottom and one on top capable of all-round fire. During the Occupation, the Germans modified it extensively, adding concrete **machine gun emplacements** around the base and on top and reinforcing floors and doorways with concrete. Today, Jersey Heritage operates the tower as a holiday let.

When first built, Archirondel Tower actually sat a little way from the shore, cut off at high water on top a rocky outcrop. The connection to the land that exists today only came about in the middle of the 19th century with the construction of what was intended to be a massive breakwater stretching into the waters of St Catherine's Bay – part of a **harbour that was never completed**.

After a number of years of peace, tensions between Britain and France were increasing once more in the 1830s and 1840s. Alarmed by the building of a huge naval base at Cherbourg, and the clear signs of other naval developments on the nearby French coast, Jersey's government pressed Britain for better protection. The result was a plan to construct a deep water **naval harbour** in the island that would enable the British fleet to remain on this side of the Channel in times of bad weather, and from where it could emerge to threaten France or defend Jersey. After some debate, the site chosen was here in St Catherine's Bay, and work commenced in 1847 on two breakwaters that when complete would create a vast enclosed harbour.

Work initially concentrated on the northern arm of the harbour, visible today across the bay from here, while the southern arm only progressed slowly. Doubts soon emerged over the wisdom of the scheme, however, as not only were costs spiralling upwards, but relations between Britain and France were also steadily improving – the countries even fought as allies in the 1854 Crimean War. Worst of all, the proposed harbour was found to silt up too easily meaning that the fleet's increasingly large warships could not enter. In 1855, after the completion of the northern arm, work stopped and plans were shelved, leaving the half-finished harbour we see today. It just goes to show that poorly thought through planning decisions are not just something that only happens today!

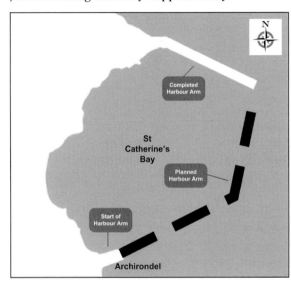

The original plan for St Catherine's Harbour, before cost, silt and peace with France left it half finished

After inspecting the rather forlorn remains of Archirondel's intended breakwater, walk back along the path to the car park at its base, noting the remains of a largely destroyed German **bunker for a tank turret** on the left, the result of rather misplaced post-Occupation demolition efforts. From the car park, turn right down the slip leading to St Catherine's beach to find a **bunker for a 7.5cm anti-tank gun** on our left, angled menacingly over the beach. This and the other German fortifications here were part of *Resistance Nest Archirondel*, which was responsible for defending this area.

A narrow coastal path starts below this bunker, which we follow walking carefully along the top of the wall around the beach, or if the path is closed climb the steps provided to reach the road which we follow until reaching the second Conway-style round tower of our walk. St Catherine's Tower is more conventional in design that its counterpart across the bay, with no gun platform at the base and the traditional four 'machiolations' around the top. Armed with a single cannon on top, it would have dominated the beach here and defended access to the road behind that leads inland.

Pressing on across the slip, the coastal path winds in front of a small and recently modernised property called 'L'Hôpital', which was once the infirmary for workers engaged in harbour construction. After a while, the path rises into some trees, and we pass an earth-covered building on the right, once possibly an ammunition store for one of several cannon batteries that stood along this shore during the Napoleonic Wars. Just after this, the coastal path ends at the main road. Ahead looms the massive evidence of quarrying here – Jersey's own 'Rock of Gibraltar'.

Much of the stone for the planned 19th century harbour came from this area, hewn out the headland that once stood here and leaving behind the massive detached rock formation now standing at the base of St Catherine's Breakwater. The evidence of that quarrying effort is obvious, as is the scale of the labours needed to extract the required amount of stone. Spare a thought for the hundreds of men who would have toiled here for several years – only to find out eventually that their work had been in vain.

Today's road circles around the rock, and we take the right-hand fork past the boat parks and sailing club until reaching the seafront. On our left, we find the fruits of a later generation of labourers, many of whom had no choice but to dig here under a harsh and often brutal regime. Set into the Gibraltar Rock is a German bunker for a 10.5cm gun. While the bunker design is a conventional one, behind there is an extensive tunnel system bored into the rock that provided both protection for the gun crew and ammunition

German bunker at St Catherine's Breakwater behind which an extensive tunnel system exists under Jersey's 'Rock of Gibraltar'

storage. Today, the complex contains a fish farm that raises turbot, and which can be visited on request.

Moving on towards the base of the breakwater and café – both of which are worthy of a visit – we find further evidence of *Resistance Nest Mole Verclut*, the German designation for the defences here. On either side of the café are two **personnel shelter bunkers**, clad in camouflaging granite, while on top of the rock at this point, there is a **searchlight platform** for a 150cm searchlight codenamed Albert. Scattered around are further minor concrete bunkers, once housing machine guns or mortars.

Leaving the breakwater behind, our walk continues around the rock, passing the public toilets on the left before taking another coastal path on the right marked by the signpost 'Footpath to Fliquet'. After a short climb, we arrive at two lines of rusty railway tracks sunk into the ground across the path. These date from the Occupation, placed here by the Germans as **anti-tank obstacles**, when the path was wider and less worn than it is today. Just after, the path splits and we take the right hand turn down to Fliquet Bay.

At Fliquet, we find the last of the towers encountered on this walk, and certainly the strangest looking of all those that remain in Jersey today. **Fliquet Tower** started life in the 1780s as a standard Conway-style round tower but at some point its top was removed and, for reasons unknown, replaced later with the one seen now, complete with decorative crenulations. During the Occupation, the Germans made further modifications, turning the tower into a **personnel shelter** complete with fortress doors that remain today. Alongside is a **bunker** for a mortar and machine gun,

Fliquet Tower, with its unusual decorative top

while a little way up the road we took to reach the tower is a **concrete platform for a 10.5cm gun**. Together, the fortifications here formed *Resistance Nest Fliquet*, responsible for defending this part of the coast.

The tower here at Fliquet is also sometimes referred to as 'Telegraph Tower', a reference to an **important wartime telephone cable** that once ran from here under the sea to France. The British military installed it during the spring of 1940 to help improve communications between the London and the British Army then serving in France. Within weeks of its commissioning, however, the cable ended up being cut as the island demilitarised before the Germans arrived. The damage inflicted was quickly repaired, however, presenting the Germans with a brand new telephone cable connecting their forces in Jersey to the Continent.

Leaving Fliquet Bay and its former cable, follow the road past the tower and round the curious granite building. The road climbs steeply for a while before levelling out for a pleasant walk. As it does, pause for a moment to consider the fields to our right, quiet and rural today, but in 1944 the site of a hastily built German artillery battery capable of dominating the waters between here and France.

Until the summer of 1944, the Germans considered the threat of an invasion on Jersey's east coast as low given the protective shelter offered by the occupied coast of France. Following D-Day and the Battle of Normandy, however, that coast fell into Allied hands, and the threat of attack from a new enemy over the water increased. In the late summer and autumn of 1944 therefore, the Germans reoriented many of the their defences in this direction, even going to the trouble of moving two powerful artillery batteries from Guernsey. One, *Battery Haeseler*, was installed in fields above La Coupe, a short distance away from where we are now. Although no trace remains today, at the start of 1945 there were four 15cm guns here with a range of over fifteen miles, surrounded by a barbed wire perimeter and defended by machine guns, mortars and anti-aircraft weapons. The 150cm searchlight on Gibraltar Rock was part of the battery, used to illuminate possible night time targets.

Moving on, in due course we arrive at a main road and turn left to walk along it past the riding stables and other buildings until seeing a sign on the right-hand side that indicates a footpath to St Catherine's

Woods. Follow the path as it plunges down into the valley, noting on the right across the fields the rather grand façade of **Rozel Manor**, standing here since the 14th century as the seat of the influential Lemprière family. During the Occupation, it was also at the centre of *Resistance Nest Rozel Manor*, an inland defensive position manned by a company of German soldiers.

Our descending footpath, which can be muddy and slippery at times, eventually reaches the valley floor and the top end of St Catherine's Woods, a long stretch of woodland managed today as a nature reserve. Turn left here to follow the marked path running through the trees alongside the meadow, noting that it may once have been a Perquage, or medieval sanctuary path, used by those accused of crimes to escape from Martin's Church to St Catherine's Bay. During the Occupation, islanders had a more basic need of the woods here at St Catherine, as a fuel crisis gripped Jersey during the last winter of the Second World War. With the Allied capture of the nearby French coast in August 1944, supplies of coal and oil to the island ceased, leaving only local stockpiles that soon ran low. In desperation, both locals and occupiers turned to wood as a means of cooking and heating, with many of Jersey's trees falling victim to the axe. By the end of the Occupation, it was estimated two hundred thousand had been felled. These woods would have been a rich source of timber, so try to imagine both civilians and soldiers hard at work here, desperately hacking or collecting the natural resources to help stay alive.

Making our way along the path leading through the valley today, there is little to remind us of those days of occupation. Yet as we reach the pretty pond near the bottom of the valley, there is one lasting and very large legacy from that time and the earlier harbour construction to consider. The pond was originally a quarry, used to extract stone for the Archirondel breakwater. It became a reservoir called La Maseline in 1943, created by a **large concrete dam** built by the Germans to provide a water source on this side of the island.

Walking past the dam, follow the track through the car park until reaching the road and crossroads a little further on. Cross over and go straight ahead along the pine tree lined La Route Le Brun opposite, until reaching the slip road down to Archirondel and the end of our walk.

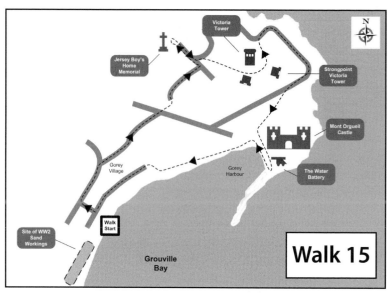

Above right: Mont Orgueil Castle, from the hill that would eventually lead to its demise

Above left: The Medieval keep of Mont Orgueil, marked out by its lighter mortar, still in place behind later fortifications and with a German artillery observation tower on top

Walk 15: Eastern Ramparts

A circular walk around and through the multi-layered military history of Gorey.

Gorey and its towering Mont Orgueil Castle must be among the best known and most featured locations in Jersey. And yet, while the castle itself rightly holds the position of prime importance, within a short distance of its ramparts are a wealth of other sites that make Gorey one of the most interesting and varied locations for military history and fortifications in the island. Their presence, and the fact that the coast of France is clearly visible just over twenty miles away, reminds us of Gorey's importance to Jersey as a first line of defence, particularly for the centuries during which the principal threat came from the island's neighbour just across the sea.

Start:	Public toilets in Long Beach Car Park
Length:	2 miles / 1.5 hours
Difficulty:	Moderate, with one steep hill to climb and descend
Getting there –	
By car:	free parking in Long Beach Car Park
By bus:	Route 1 runs from Liberation Station, alighting at Long Beach Car Park
Refreshments:	Several restaurants, bars and cafés in Gorey Village and Harbour
Amenities:	Public toilets at Long Beach Car Par and Gorey Harbour

From the public toilets here in Long Beach Car Park, the wide beach of Grouville is just a short distance away. Given its proximity to France and the fact that behind lies the wide and open Grouville Common, a threat of invasion hung over this area for centuries. As a result, the bay was strongly defended, not only by Mont Orgueil Castle, which we visit later on this walk, but also by a number of smaller fortifications. Most are still present, with many visited on Walk 16, but one in particular has rather mysteriously disappeared.

Tower No. 8 was the last of six Conway-style round towers (being the eighth of eight fortifications in Grouville Bay, not just towers), built between La Rocque and Gorey and which once stood on the foreshore somewhere near these toilets. It remained there until at least 1849 but was gone by the start of the 20th century, possibly demolished when Gorey Station was built here in 1872, although there is also a report suggesting that the vibrations of passing trains may have weakened its structure. Either way, the beach is somewhat diminished without what would have been an impressive landmark.

The beach here should also be considerably diminished when it comes to sand, given the amount taken from it during the Occupation by the Germans to build their huge array of fortifications. Following an island survey in 1941, German engineers identified the sand of Grouville Bay as being the right type for their concrete and in sufficient quantity to meet construction requirements. As a result, a sprawling **works of machinery, railways and roads** was established on Grouville Common to extract the sand from the beach, gather it in huge mounds and then load it onto transports for carrying around the island. One such mound filled the car park next to the toilets here, with a road and railway running alongside allowing the almost continuous collection of sand. By mid-1943, when construction efforts were scaled back, it was estimated that one million tons of sand had been excavated – although remarkably, the beach appeared to have returned to normal by 1946.

Walk from the toilets to the main road, noting the former Jersey Eastern Railway buildings immediately on the right. Cross the main road and walk straight ahead into Gorey Village, turning right at the T-junction to pass Roseville Stores and later the Old Bank House

Hotel. Just after this, the road forks and we take the right hand road up towards Gouray Church on the hillside above. Upon reaching the next junction, cross the main road and turn right, walking on the pavement down the hill. After around twenty metres, a granite-coined entrance appears on the left, leading to a steep, but thankfully quite short, set of steps. Go up and then continue right along the tarmac road that gently climbs higher to bring the castle and bay into view. Stop at the top of the road, perhaps taking a well-earned rest on the one of the benches here, and take in the magnificent vista of castle, harbour and the Royal Bay of Grouville, the latter title being gained following a visit by Queen Victoria in 1846.

From this spot, the attraction of the bay to an invader is obvious, especially if he is coming from France, which is usually visible across the sea. Since just after 1204, when King John of England lost control of his Norman lands but retained the Channel Islands, Mont Orgueil Castle has stood here as a prominent deterrent against any such invasion. From the time of its construction until the end of the 17th century, the castle was Jersey's principal fortification, undergoing many changes in that time to adapt to the evolving challenges of warfare. From this vantage point we can gain a brief understanding of those changes and identify the three main phases of fortification development seen today.

Archaeological evidence suggests that the promontory above Gorey Harbour was a defended place as far back as the Iron Age, with ditches and earth ramparts present here three thousand years ago. The earliest fortifications seen today are those of King John's original medieval castle, built to a traditional concentric pattern with a keep – today partially visible at the rear of the highest part of the castle – protected by **walls, towers and gates** manned by defenders wielding swords, shields, bows and arrows. The fact the castle sits on a high promontory surrounded on three sides by sea and cliffs added to its extraordinary defensive capabilities during this period.

Yet the advent of gunpowder and cannon from the 14th century onwards gradually undermined this advantage, and exposed the castle's weakness. Cannon placed on the hill on which we are now standing could dominate the castle, having the range and height advantage needed to pound it into submission. Unwilling to give up a fortification that had served them so well, however, in the Tudor period a comprehensive remodelling of the castle took place, building the angular **Grand Battery** we see jutting out toward the hill opposite and constructing the enormous half-round **Somerset Tower** in front of the medieval keep to absorb cannon fire. From the top of the latter, cannon could also dominate this hill opposite.

In the end, however, it was a forlorn effort, and the mantle of principal defence moved to the more modern Elizabeth Castle outside St Helier Harbour. Mont Orgueil Castle, while retaining some of its weaponry, became a second-line fortification, used mainly as a prison and barracks. At one time, there was even a plan to demolish it before the then governor, Walter Raleigh, stepped in to save the old castle, saying "twere pity to cast it down".

Its military use was not quite over, however, as during the Second World War came a third phase of development. The Germans built three **artillery observation towers** on top, although a careful use of granite is testament to the efforts made to blend them into their surroundings. Look carefully to see if they can be identified.

Turning our back on the castle, which we inspect more closely later on, walk inland on the tarmac drive until we reach the main road. Continue straight along this for about fifty metres until reaching the entrance to a large and rather austere granite-fronted building on the left, in front of which is a memorial. Stop here.

The building today is an accommodation and activity centre, but Haut de la Garenne, as it is called, opening in 1867 as an industrial school for 'young people of the lower classes of society and neglected children'. In its more recent history, it has the dubious distinction of being at the centre of a child abuse scandal that engulfed the island in controversy. In 1914, however, it was the Jersey Home for Boys and this **war memorial** commemorates the 33 former pupils who died fighting for King and Country during the First World War. Among them are two brothers, **Alfred and William Woonton**, of the Jersey Contingent, who died in 1917 and 1918 respectively, seaman **Otto Drube**, who was killed at Battle of Jutland while serving on HMS *Black Prince*, and **Cyril Sollet**, captured in Mesopotamia in April

Jersey Boys Home memorial to its dead of the First World War

1916 and who died as a Turkish prisoner-of-war four months later. Pause for a moment and consider the number of names for a relatively small institution, and then the impact of that war on a small island such as Jersey.

Leaving Haut de la Garenne, retrace our steps back toward Gorey but remain on the main road as it bends left. On the bend, we find a turning right onto the road / track with a sign marked 'private road'. After walking some 200 metres along it, we arrive at a mass of modern aerials and communication masts sitting on top of a concrete bunker.

This was originally built by the Germans as an **artillery observation bunker** with two granite-clad lookout posts visible today on the top facing north and south. After the Occupation, however, unlike most of its contemporaries, this bunker had a later defence role as a **Cold War** monitoring station, used to measure the amount of radiation present following a nuclear exchange. Thankfully, it was never needed, and the bunker became home to some of the communications equipment now required to keep the island covered in mobile phone and radio signals.

Continue past the bunker with the aerials into the small car park. To our left lies Victoria Tower, which we shall visit shortly, but in the meantime, take the path on the right hand side of the car park and follow it round until Mont Orgueil Castle comes clearly into view. From here, it is truly possible to appreciate its vulnerability from cannon mounted on this hill. We are also now in the heart of *Strongpoint Victoria Tower*, an important German defensive position during the Occupation, particularly after June 1944.

Up until D-Day on 6 June 1944, the east of the island was considered less threatened due to the protection offered by the nearby and German occupied coast of France. After it fell to the advancing Americans in August 1944, however, the Germans began reinforcing this part of the island. One addition was a large **radar installation**, brought across from France and set up here in September 1944. Further developments around Victoria Tower included a number of 2cm anti-aircraft guns, one of which was mounted on the tower itself, and a powerful 150cm searchlight for illuminating targets during the night time. Other fortifications included **personnel shelter bunkers** and **mortar bunkers**, now mostly buried or lost in the undergrowth, and a **machine gun emplacement** visible a little way down the slope towards the castle.

Following the path around the headland, we arrive at wonderfully situated **Victoria Tower**, the last coastal defence tower built in Jersey, and to a unique design that includes a moat and drawbridge. Its erection here in 1837 served to both protect the vulnerable approaches to Mont

Victoria Tower, the last coastal defence tower built in Jersey

Orgueil Castle, and deter landings in Anne Port Bay lying below. Originally, its armament was a single 24-pounder cannon mounted on the roof and capable of all-round fire. Today it belongs to the National Trust for Jersey and is available for hire to the public.

Facing towards the sea and Anne Port Bay, walk down the slope from Victoria Tower to find the top of a winding footpath that descends to the road below. Here we turn right, and follow it round past Le Saut Geffroy, or Geoffroy's Leap, until Mont Orgueil Castle comes into view once more, taking very special care as the road winds without a pavement. Cross the castle green, complete with its humps and bumps, towards the entrance gate; go through to pass the impressive remains of the 15th century **Harliston Tower** on the left.

Built during a time of transition, it exemplifies the dilemma faced by the castle's designers and defender, with both slits for bow and arrow and an early gun port for a cannon.

Follow the road, or chemin, towards the castle's second gate, noting the medieval curtain walls towering above us on the left-hand side. Stop outside the ticket office which, if you intend visiting the castle, you must pay to enter. There are options for guided or self-guided tours, with either recommended. If you are continuing on this walk, take the small set of steps opposite the ticket office down through the Postern Gate and into the **Outer Ward**.

For many years, this part of the castle was inaccessible and overgrown. In medieval times, it was an enclosed area, or Outer Ward, protected by a wall perhaps studded with towers running along where the houses of Gorey Harbour now stand. It may have held livestock together with a well, the remains of which can be seen near the ruins of a 16th century 'half-moon battery' built in this part of the castle. Follow the path through the Outer Ward to steps that lead down to a granite-flagged platform sited at the base of Gorey Harbour Pier.

We have reached the **Water Battery**, built during the Napoleonic Wars with its cannon defending the marine approaches to Gorey Harbour. During the Occupation, the Germans added defences of their own here, part of *Resistance Nest Hafen Gorey*, a **machine gun emplacement** and a **bunker for a tank turret** equipped with an anti-tank gun remain to be seen.

Leaving the Water Battery via the steps to the pier, turn right noting that the second dwelling along has some unusual features within its façade. During the Occupation, it housed a machine gun behind the loophole on the ground floor while on the first floor balcony there was a 3.7cm anti-tank gun.

Continue along the pier until it joins the shore, with plenty of refreshment options in this area if required. Our walk now follows the seafront path back to Long Beach Car Park, although note that the coach park for Gorey now covers the site once filled by a large German bunker for a **7.5cm anti-tank gun**, which was demolished in 1972.

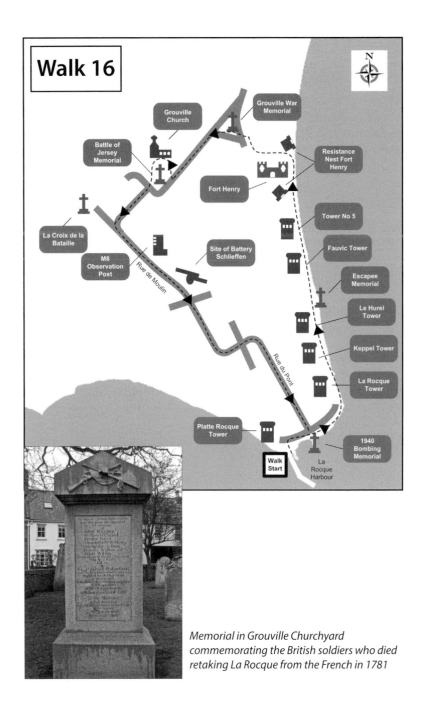

Walk 16

N

Grouville Church

Grouville War Memorial

Battle of Jersey Memorial

Resistance Nest Fort Henry

Fort Henry

Tower No 5

La Croix de la Bataille

Fauvic Tower

M8 Observation Post

Site of Battery Schlieffen

Escapee Memorial

Rue de Moulin

Le Hurel Tower

Keppel Tower

Rue du Pont

La Rocque Tower

Platte Rocque Tower

Walk Start

La Rocque Harbour

1940 Bombing Memorial

Memorial in Grouville Churchyard commemorating the British soldiers who died retaking La Rocque from the French in 1781

Walk 16: The Eight Towers

A long walk from La Rocque Harbour to Grouville Common before turning inland for a visit to Grouville Church and Mill.

La Rocque is probably the location where Jersey's remarkable tidal range has the most pronounced impact on the local panorama, with a vast wilderness of sand and rocks appearing at low tide. It could be presumed that all these rocks makes the area an unlikely place to invade Jersey, yet as we discover, the area is steeped in military history, including probably the best known invasion in the island's past. This act and the threat of invasion before and subsequently, kept this part of Jersey on high alert for hundreds of years, with the evidence clearly visible on a long but satisfying walk.

Start:	La Rocque Harbour Pier
Length:	5 miles / 3.5 hours
Difficulty:	Easy, with one moderate hill to climb and descend.

Note: *try to coincide the start of the walk with low tide in order to avoid a busy road and gain best views*

Getting there –	
By car:	Free parking at La Rocque Harbour although in the summer it can become full
By bus:	Route 1 from Liberation Station, alighting at La Rocque Harbour
Refreshments:	Beach café at La Rocque (seasonal), pub serving food near entrance to Royal Jersey Golf Course
Amenities:	Public Toilets at La Rocque Harbour

Our walk starts a little way along the pier, where a **commemorative tablet** recalls the landing here of a French force under Baron De Rullecourt on the night of 5th / 6th January 1781.

This was of course the start of events that would end in St Helier's Royal Square with the Battle of Jersey, and the deaths of both Major Peirson, who led the island's forces, and De Rullecourt. The square is visited on Walk No 1, and the story of the events that day are covered in the Brief History at the start of this book, so we won't recall all the detail now. Considering that night more than two hundred years ago, however, it should be noted that neither the pier nor the Conway-style round tower standing above us was present then. The same is true of **Seymour Tower,** visible out from the end of the pier a mile offshore, although there may have been an earlier fortification on its site when the French landed that night. Seymour Tower, which is Jersey's only 'square' coastal tower and now a holiday let, went up in its present form in 1782, the year after the Battle of Jersey.

Above: Plaque recalling De Rullecourt's landing at La Rocque in 1781 before his march on St Helier

Left: The Baron De Rullecourt, who landed at La Rocque in 1781, dreamt of conquering Jersey but ended up meeting his death instead

Turning back to La Rocque, the **Platte Rocque Tower** here was built in the years following the Battle of Jersey, possibly between 1793 and 1795 on this raised piece of land known as La Platte Rocque. Prior to that, a small fortification stood on or near this point, which was taken easily by the French in 1781 and left defended by around a hundred men while the main force marched on St Helier. Later that day, a force of regular British soldiers and men from the Jersey Militia attacked and defeated the small French detachment, with a number of the British soldiers killed. Later in the walk, we discover more about their final resting place.

During the Occupation, the Germans fortified La Platte Rocque and the harbour area to form *Resistance Nest La Rocque A*, with several machine guns, including one on top of the tower, a bunker for a 5cm anti-tank gun, a bunker for a tank turret and a searchlight position. The remains of these are on private land around the tower, although some outlines are visible from the pier wall. On the pier itself there were two bunkers for tank turrets, of which only one remains at the very end.

Walking back to the road we turn right and follow the pavement until reaching the next slip. At its top, there is a memorial tablet, this time recalling the events of 28 June 1940 when German bombers swept in here from France on their way to attack St Helier. The German pilots did not know the island was demilitarised by then, and had orders to find out the level of preparations made by any defenders. Making land here, they dropped bombs and fired machine guns at people below. The attack was over in seconds, but as we see from the memorial, it sadly left three civilians dead.

Continuing away from La Rocque, it makes sense to climb down onto the beach upon reaching the first houses on the seaward side of the road – if the tide is out. Although a narrow path exists in front of the houses above the beach, it stops after a short while. As an alternative, we could walk along the road, but it is usually busy with traffic and mostly lacks a pavement. Walking a little way down the beach, on the other hand, allows for a much better appreciation of the several towers along this part of the coast, the first of which soon comes into view.

This is Tower No. 1, or La Rocque Tower, the second Conway-style round tower passed on our walk. Around its base was located *Resistance Nest La Rocque B*, created by the Germans to defend the coast here with two 10.5cm guns, one of which was in a fortified shelter overlooking the beach, two bunkers for tank-turrets, and machine guns and searchlights. The remains today are on private property.

Continuing along the beach, we pass Tower No. 2 (Keppel Tower) and **Tower No. 3 (Le Hurel) Tower**, both of which are also Conway-style round towers incorporated today into private dwellings. In front of Tower No 2, there are some granite blocks engraved with W↑D, indicated the land's former ownership by the British War Department. Just after Tower No 3, we reach Fauvic Slip, and another **memorial tablet** on the right, this time commemorating wartime escapees.

In August 1944, the German forces in Jersey, and the island's inhabitants became isolated when American forces liberated the French coast opposite following D-Day and the Battle of Normandy. The thought that liberty was within sight was too much for many local young men who resolved to cross the stretch of water to France. This place, known as the **Fauvic Embarkation Point** was a popular location to start the journey. Living nearby in a farm called Belair were members of the Bertram family, who gave special assistance to many by concealing the small boats used for the crossing, together with fuel and supplies. More than fifty people left Jersey from this point, a high percentage of approximately one hundred and forty who attempted to escape, including the late Sir Peter Crill, the former Bailiff who unveiled this memorial.

The escapes here happened under the noses of the German, who in fact had *Operational Point Le Hurel* within a few metres from the slip and today marked by the granite-clad protrusion from the sea wall, once a **bunker for a tank turret** armed with an anti-tank gun. Walking on again along the beach we soon reach **Tower No. 4 (Fauvic Tower)**, again converted into a rather impressive property. Just beyond, steps leading up from the beach take us to a wide path running along the top of the seawall. On the top of this wall, we encounter two further **memorials to wartime escapees**, including one recalling Victor Huelin, Robert Woods and Harry McFarlane. Although they made it across the France successfully, landing at Surville-sur-Mer, it's worth recalling that others did not. Most escapes took place in the winter of 1944/45 under cover of darkness, hardly an ideal season to set out in a small boat for the hazardous crossing. Not only did they have heavy seas, strong tides and hidden rocks to contend with, but also hostile and jumpy occupying forces often ready to open fire on any suspicious craft. As a result, at least ten escapees lost their lives during this period of the Occupation.

Pressing on, we come to **Tower No. 5**, the last of the five towers built between La Rocque and Grouville Common, and the sixth we have passed on this walk so far. Even today, surrounded by built-up development, the five towers along this stretch of the coast remain an impressive sight when viewed from a little way down the beach, silent sentinels to Jersey's historic and often turbulent relationship with her nearest neighbour.

Unlike most of its counterparts along this part of the coast, Tower No. 5 stands empty and some-what dilapidated

Just before we reach the fairways, flags and greens of the Jersey Royal Golf Club, whose course fills much of Grouville Common today, there is the matter of the **Grouville Concentration Camp** to consider. The camp, which occupied the site now covered in houses next to the golf course, started life in the 1930s as the Grouville Holiday Camp, offering inexpensive family holidays. On the outbreak of war, however, the British Army took over its holiday huts as an internment camp for enemy nationals caught in Jersey at the start of hostilities. Surrounded by barbed wire and guarded by soldiers, it became the Grouville Concentration Camp, a name not yet synonymous with the Nazi labour and death camps. After the Germans arrived in 1940, the camp was used to house French, North African and Spanish forced labourers being employed at the German sand producing works on the common. Ironically, given that the Spanish inmates were republicans who had fled fascist Spain, the camp was renamed Lager Franco after the Spanish dictator.

Continuing and passing the start of the golf course on our left, the very obvious granite walls and tower (our seventh) of **Fort Henry** appears, set back just a little way from the beach. It stands on a site fortified since the 15th century, although the current buildings date from the mid-18th century. During the Battle of Jersey, British troops stationed here (it was called Fort Conway at the time) took part in the victorious attack on the French force that remained at Platte Rocque. In the years that followed, it was garrisoned according to the threat of war, with cannon situated on the tower and, inside the walls, barracks used by generations of British soldiers. When the First World War broke out in 1914, it became home to members of the 2nd (East) Battalion of the Jersey Militia, who roofed the tower for a while. The militia also used a rifle range then situated on the common to the north of the fort, but which was later lost as golf took over.

During the Occupation, a redeveloped fort emerged at the heart of a prominent defensive position once more, named by the Germans *Resistance Nest Fort Henry*. In the fort itself, the German-built concrete **machine gun emplacements** on the two corners overlooking the beach and a third on top of the tower. Inside the walls they constructed a **personnel shelter bunker**, while the tower itself housed a 60cm searchlight at first floor level that could emerge onto either of the two projecting 'balconies', which were added at the time but camouflaged by granite-cladding. Outside the walls, a number of bunkers were built, linked back to the fort by a trench that passed beneath its walls. Two of these are clearly visible today overlooking the beach. Both are **bunkers for 10.5cm guns**, one angled to fire back along the beach towards La Rocque, the other towards Gorey Harbour.

Our walk continues past the first, below which there is a granite-clad **machine gun emplacement**, and on to the second, noting that we are now on top of a German **anti-tank wall**, designated PzM9 (*PzM standing for Panzermauern or anti-tank wall*). From the second bunker, we can walk to the walls of Fort Henry, taking great care to avoid flying golf balls as we cross the common and its fairways. Passing the fort, note the raised lump of ground on our right, which is the buried remains of a small **mortar bunker**. A little further away, under the 14th green, are the shattered remains of a **heavy machine gun bunker** that once mounted a massive steel turret for two machine guns, but was mostly demolished after the Occupation.

Walk round the fort's walls to reach its entrance. From here we walk smartly across the path to the road, again watching out for flying balls and respecting those for whom the local fortifications will always be secondary to a round of golf. Follow the road as it leads away from Fort Henry, noting that during the Occupation, a vast sand extraction and storage scheme filled the common here, with the details covered more fully on Walk 15. We reach the main road next to a splendid statue of famous Jersey golfer Harry Vardon. To our left is the Pembroke pub, which could be a place to stop for refreshments, while to our right and across the main road, is the **Grouville War Memorial**, which is the next stop on our walk.

Like most others in the island, the memorial here was erected after the First World War to commemorate the parish of Grouville's dead from that conflict. Further names were added following the Second World War, although far fewer, indicating the scale of the island's loss during the first great conflict of the 20th century. Among the many engraved names are a group of *Ancienne Combattant Français*, who were French nationals living and working in Jersey but who returned to serve with their regiments when war broke out in August 1914. They include three Leverdiers, or Le Verdiers, who appear to have been brothers, while among the local names are those of Harold and Keith Simonet, both sons of a distinguished Grouville family who lived at Radier Manor. Directly opposite the front panel of the memorial is a building that was once the local railway station and today is a private house. It is poignant to think it may have been the place from where local families waved off some of the men now on the memorial, without knowing they would never return.

Leaving the memorial, walk up Rue Des Pres which leads inland from the coastal road. After a short distance, we reach a main road and turn left toward Grouville Church, the spire of which is visible in the distance. Upon reaching the church, enter the churchyard via the first main gate and look for a large granite memorial among the headstones on our left.

The **memorial commemorates the seven British soldiers who fell during the fighting at Platte Rocque in 1781**. Renovated twice, it originally stood a short distance away to mark the location of their graves, but was moved to accommodate building works. An annual memorial service is held here on the anniversary of the battle, attended in recent years by a local re-enactment group dressed in period costume and bearing replica muskets. Note that the fallen soldiers commemorated here belonged to the 83rd Regiment of Foot, a British unit with links to the Royal Irish Rifles. Inside Grouville Church, a further **memorial** close to the main door recalls another link to this regiment, this time to a group of Jerseymen who served with it during the First World War.

The volunteers of the Jersey Overseas Contingent left the island in 1915 to serve in the British Army, becoming the Jersey Company of the Royal Irish Rifles. After training in Ireland, they fought in many of the war's major battles, including the Battle of the Somme and Passchendaele, suffering the loss of one in four of their number before its end in November 1918. Their link to Grouville Church comes through Arthur Durrell, the last president of their post-war association, who was an active member of the congregation here and who arranged for the erection of this memorial in 1961. Nearby in a small cabinet there should be a book inscribed with the volunteers' names, with the page still regularly turned to ensure no one is forgotten.

Elsewhere in the church are found other wartime memorials, including a remarkable wooden cross that once stood in France to mark the grave of Second Lieutenant Edward Du Faye, a local man killed in the Battle of Cambrai while serving in the newly formed Royal Tank Corps. Despite the presence of this cross, his wartime grave was subsequently lost leaving Edward commemorated today on the memorial to the missing of that battle.

Leaving the Church by the front door and gate, turn right and walk a short distance before crossing over to climb La Rue des Alleurs, the hill that starts beside the Parish Hall and which is also referred to as 'Blood Hill'. As we reach the top, the reference become clearer as on the right is a small triangle of tree-filled land complete with an old well, reportedly commemorating a battle fought here in 1406.

In that year, an army of around one thousand raiders landed on the sands outside St Helier to fight a bitter battle with a local force, which included members of the Jersey Militia. After narrowly overcoming the resistance there, the raiders, led by a Castilian nobleman called Pero Niño, reputedly marched inland to fight another bitter battle here on Grouville Hill that was apparently so fierce that blood ran freely down its sides. After this, the islanders agreed to pay off Niño, who left having got what he came for. How much fact lies behind this second battle is uncertain, but the long-held view is that the triangle of land here, and known as 'La Croix de la Bataille', is associated with it.

Turning away from the trees, we walk south down Rue de Moulin à Vent, or road of the windmill. The reason for the name soon become obvious as the slender tower of a windmill appears ahead – the eighth and final tower of our walk – although this is a windmill with a difference.

Formerly called Grouville Mill, the Germans converted it into an **artillery observation position** during the Occupation, designated M8 (*M standing for Meßstelle or Range-finding Position*), by the addition of a concrete lookout post on top. Standing today near its base, the reason for the conversion is obvious with the mill, which is now a private house, providing commanding views over Gorey and Grouville Bay. In August 1944, it took on a further role, becoming the observation and command post for Battery Schlieffen, a heavy coastal artillery unit moved from Guernsey to bolster Jersey's eastern defences after the nearby French coast had fallen to the American Army. The four 15cm guns of **Battery Schlieffen** were installed in rudimentary emplacements among fields to the left of the road just past the mill.

With a range of over fifteen miles, they could dominate the eastern approaches to Jersey. Nothing now remains here, with the heavy guns dumped over the cliffs at Les Landes after the Occupation. One 15cm gun, possibly belonging to Battery Schlieffen,

One of the 15cm guns of Battery Schlieffen near Grouville Mill, brought to Jersey in 1944 to bolster east coast defences (CIOS Collection)

was however recovered from its resting place some years back, and today is on display at Noirmont Point, and visited on Walk 3.

Continuing, take the left-hand Rue de Crèvecoeur at the fork ahead, and at the bottom carefully cross the main road to follow Rue Des Nouettes until its end. Here bear right, following La Rue au Tchian and Rue du Pont until La Rocque and our starting point is reached again.

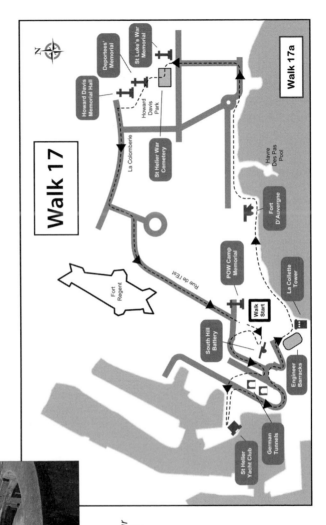

Walk 17

Walk 17a

- Deportees' Memorial
- St Luke's War Memorial
- Howard Davis Memorial Hall
- Howard Davis Park
- St Helier War Cemetery
- La Colomberie
- Fort Regent
- Rue de l'Est
- South Hill Battery
- POW Camp Memorial
- Fort D'Auvergne
- Havre Des Pas Pool
- Walk Start
- La Collette Tower
- Engineer Barracks
- St Helier Yacht Club
- German Tunnels

A British then German gun emplacement on South Hill, overlooking St Helier Harbour and Elizabeth Castle beyond

158

Walk 17: Lest we Forget

A circular walk around the east of St Helier to include visits to South Hill, Havre Des Pas and Howard Davis Park.

The eastern quarter of town is quieter in comparison to the west, being mainly residential in nature. Found here also is an unsightly, but required, collection of industrial buildings and installations situated in a bulge of reclaimed land that now covers much of the area's former foreshore. Fortunately, while this modern development may have altered the landscape, it has left intact much of its military history. This rich heritage, both on the shoreline and inland, is the subject of this walk when we discover some of St Helier's earliest and latest fortifications, Jersey's largest war memorial and the island's only military cemetery.

Start:	Mount Bingham Car Park
Length:	2 miles / 1.5 hours
Difficulty:	Easy
Getting there –	
By car:	Disc and scratch card parking at Mount Bingham.
By bus:	The start is within walking distance of Liberation Station
Refreshments:	Plenty of choice en route
Amenities:	Several public toilets en route

This walk starts in the small car park above the children's playground on Mount Bingham. Before setting off, however, we should take a moment to consider the setting, and its obvious proximity to and relationship with nearby **Fort Regent**.

Although the fort is the dominant feature on Le Mont de la Ville, which is the name for the area of high ground above town, it was only part of a far larger military complex which encompassed more than thirty acres of land in total. As well as Fort Regent, there were detached fortifications and military installations including a martello tower, barracks, married quarters, a military prison and sloping grass fields, or glacis, such as the one we can see stretching up to the derelict swimming pool on Fort Regent. We shall see some of these, or the remains of them, on our walk today. It is also worth noting that this area was the focus of considerable quarrying activity in the last two centuries, leaving some of the odd shaped lumps and bumps we see today. Our walk starts by climbing up one of those odd shaped lumps – South Hill.

Go through the gates at the end of the car park, noting the plaque on the gatepost explaining the former use of this hill, and walk up the road. The complex of office buildings below us to the right are on the site of a **former military prison**, built by the British in the 19th century, but also used by the Germans during the Occupation. Traces of it remain in the shape of older-looking granite buildings and walls. Soon we reach the top of the hill.

The South Hill site contains a remarkable and somewhat confusing range of fortifications from several eras, mostly heaped one atop another. Immediately in front as we arrive at the top of the access road is a dressed granite wall, most probably **part of a redoubt, or small fortification**, constructed here about twenty years before work commenced on Fort Regent in 1806. Turning right and past the back of the small house, we find a concrete façade, with doors and windows, and steps leading up to two concrete **gun emplacements**. This is the substantial remains of **South Hill Battery**, a British artillery installation built in the years leading up the First World War for two six-inch guns capable of firing shells at targets nearly nine miles away. The battery, which was the last operational British one in the island, was manned throughout the First World War firing regular test rounds out to sea – following suitable newspaper warnings of course.

Climb the steps to the emplacements, noting the remains of shell hoists in the floor behind them and storage niches for ammunition waiting to be loaded and fired. The battery was disarmed in 1929 and the guns removed but, during the Occupation, the Germans re-used the emplacements, installing two four-barrel, 2cm anti-aircraft guns, although these were later moved elsewhere. Other German weapons here included two 7.5cm ex-French guns and two machine guns, all of which constituted part of *Resistance Nest South Hill Oben*. In one of the emplacements we find what looks like concrete flower planters, one of which has the inscription in German, denoting its wartime occupants. In front of the emplacements, overlooking the La Collette reclamation site, is a German split-level **artillery observation bunker,** designated M9 (*M standing for Meßstelle or Range-finding Position*), while down the slope to the right, is a lawned area of humps and bumps, marking the **buried remains of generations of other fortifications** dating from the late 17th century to the Occupation.

Leaving South Hill, we retrace our steps down the access road and turn left at the car park to follow the main road around the playground and in front of the offices to reach a rather complex junction of four roads. Cross here toward the harbour, taking the steps almost in front down to reach the quayside. Cross the road and walk down South Pier opposite until the reaching St Helier Yacht Club overlooking the harbour where we stop for a moment.

Since its formation in 1903, the St Helier Yacht Club has been a stalwart champion of sailing in the island, with many achievements and highpoints to its credit. One of the most notable came in June 1940, as German forces approached the French port of St Malo, threatening to trap thousands of British and Canadian soldiers there. Following a request by the British Admiralty, the Club organised a flotilla of small boats that sailed from St Helier Harbour to help with the evacuation – later known as the 'Little Dunkirk'. In recognition of this brave deed, it was awarded a unique 'Battle Honour', the right to fly a Red Ensign flag 'defaced' with an anchor and crossed axes emblem. Within weeks of the evacuation, however, the Germans arrived in Jersey and St Helier harbour became a key facility for the occupying forces. The building that today houses the Yacht Club became part of the harbour defences, converted to hold a machine gun and protected by a steel armoured door, which can be seen today underneath the external staircase.

The 'Defaced Red Ensign' of the St Helier Yacht Club, an honour bestowed in recognition of its members' efforts in 1940

Walk back down the pier to the main road and turn right. In the rock face opposite are the concrete entrances of two tunnels, built by the Germans during the Occupation. The first, designated HO19 (*HO standing for Hohlgangslagen, or cave passage installation*), was constructed to hold a large electricity generator that would have powered the harbour cranes in an emergency. The second, which clearly enters the hillside at an angle, was a tunnel through which a narrow-gauge railway ran to transport building materials between St Helier and Gorey.

Cross over the road and continue, passing a plaque commemorating men from Jersey that fought in the Burma Campaign, and noting the memorial to the philanthropic Westaway sisters and a second recalling the wreck of mail steamer *Normandy* in 1870. Follow the road up behind the memorials, crossing again to take the small steps before continuing with the modern day power station below us on the right. Note that on top of the heights to our left there are the dressed granite remains of some of South Hill's earliest fortifications, probably dating back to the second half of the 18th century. Where the pavement ends, turn right to follow the road around the power station and then left to stop in front of the collection of buildings here, today used by the Ministry of Defence as headquarters for the Jersey Field Squadron. In response to British pressure for a contribution towards the cost of the island's defence, in 1987 Jersey agreed to form a field squadron of engineers, which would be part of the British Territorial Army. The unit, which has sent members to serve in many modern conflicts including Bosnia, Iraq and Afghanistan, took on the lineage of the Jersey Militia, thus resurrecting a tradition dating back hundreds of years.

The buildings, known as the **Engineer Barracks**, are part of the huge Napoleonic Wars era military complex with Fort Regent at its centre. Walking past their gate, we reach the pretty La Collette Gardens. To the right we can inspect the outer walls of the barracks, complete with musket loopholes. Follow the line of this wall towards the round tower at its end. **La Collette Tower**, which is also known as Pointe des Pas, dates to 1834 and is built in true martello style – note the strong design contrast to Jersey's more numerous Conway-style round towers – with a 24-pounder cannon formerly mounted in an emplacement on top. During the Occupation, the Germans modified the emplacement to accommodate a four-barrel, 2cm anti-aircraft gun, part of *Resistance Nest Südfort*, which also included the rather rudimentary **machine gun emplacement** close to the tower's base. This is reached by walking round the tower, although its firing slit today faces reclaimed land and the island's incinerator.

Leaving the tower and barracks, walk through the gardens, taking steps on the right leading down to reach the promenade that runs around Havre Des Pas Beach. Here we are on the former track of the German railway once more. Follow it round to the slip, where there is a small **bunker for a tank turret**, once armed with a 3.7cm anti-tank gun, part of *Resistance Nest de la Plage*. Note the use of granite as camouflage. The slip is opposite a road called Green Street. Looking towards it from here, note the modern housing development on the left hand side, now covering the location of an extensive **soldiers' married quarters** once associated with the Mont de la Ville military complex and which were demolished in the 1960s. Also across the main road here, and a little way up the hill, is a **plaque denoting that T E Lawrence, or Lawrence of Arabia** as he is better known, lived here as a young boy with his family.

Continuing on our walk, follow the promenade, passing a memorial garden dedicated to the shipyards that once dominated this part of St Helier. Near the public bathing pool, the promenade turns sharply to the left and we find a plaque recalling the small **Fort D'Auvergne** that once stood on this point.

Continue along the pleasant seafront where, after passing the bridge leading to Havre Des Pas Swimming Pool, we reach a row of properties between the road and beach, one of which had a notorious reputation during the Occupation. The Silvertide Guest House, now a building divided into flats, was commandeered from 1943 as headquarters for the local *Geheime Feldpolizei* or Secret Field Police, whose role was to watch over both the civilian population and military forces in the island, dealing with acts of espionage, sabotage, treason, etc. Anyone suspected of illicit activities of this nature was brought to Silvertide for interrogation, and many found themselves transported to camps and installations in Germany where some met their deaths.

Continuing on to the T-junction with small painted roundabout, we follow the road right past the shops, public house and slip to the beach. As the road straightens once more, between it and the beach is a modern apartment building, which was once the location of the Victor Hugo Hotel, another building with something of a reputation during the Occupation. The Germans requisitioned it for use as their 'Forces Brothel', an establishment staffed by French girls and very popular with the troops by all accounts. Cross over here, to take Beach Road away from the coast. Crossing one road, continue until the main road at the top at which point we cross over to enter Howard Davis Park using the gates next to St Luke's Anglican Church. Before going into the park itself, turn right before the church to visit its **War Memorial**.

The memorial commemorates the ecclesiastical parish war dead, mainly men from the First World War, among them a C Laugeard. **Sergeant Charles Laugeard**, who was a policeman before the war, joined the Jersey Contingent in 1915, winning the Distinguished Conduct Medal (DCM) in September 1916 during the Battle of the Somme. At the start of 1918, he married the recently widowed Lillian Mason, whose husband had been a fellow policeman and friend prior to the war. Sadly for Lillian, Sergeant Laugeard was killed in October 1918, just a few weeks before the war ended, leaving her twice widowed by the same conflict.

Leave the churchyard, and enter the war cemetery across the

path. The **St Helier War Cemetery** was first opened in 1943 by the Germans to bury the bodies of British servicemen washed ashore on the island's coast. Most of them came from the Royal Navy ships HMS *Charybdis* and HMS *Limbourne*, which were sunk in October 1943 during a battle off the nearby French coast with the loss of more than 500 lives. The bodies that came ashore in Jersey were initially buried elsewhere, before a decision in November 1943 to reinter them here in Howard Davis Park, along with the remains of three Royal Air force men already buried in the island. The service took place with full military honours accorded to the deceased, and in the presence of many islanders who came to pay their respects.

Left: Sergeant Charles Laugeard DCM of the Jersey Contingent who died only weeks before the end of the First World War, and who is today commemorated on the St Luke's Church War Memorial

Right: The grave of Maurice Gould, whose remains were brought to the war cemetery in Howard Davis Park from their resting place in Germany

Later, the bodies of other Allied servicemen were buried here, including a number of American sailors and airmen, although their remains were moved to a US cemetery in France after the war. The same is true for Squadron Leader Gonray, a Belgian airman killed while serving in the RAF, who was moved to a family grave in Belgium. Also in the cemetery is the grave of Private Hanlon, a British First World War soldier who died in 1916 while serving in the island, and whose remains were moved here from St Brelade's

Churchyard during the Occupation to make way for a German cemetery there. Finally, in a somewhat solitary grave rests Maurice Gould, a Jersey civilian caught by the Germans in 1942 while trying to escape the island. After finding that Maurice and his friend Peter Hassell had information on them deemed militarily sensitive, both were sent for torture and imprisonment in concentration camps on the Continent where Maurice died of tuberculosis in October 1943. Peter Hassell survived to return home, but on discovering years later that Maurice was interred among German soldiers, campaigned to have his friend's body returned to Jersey. This finally happened in 1997, with this cemetery chosen to receive the remains.

Walk through the cemetery, turning right at the dedication stone to go through the gate on the right hand side. A short distance along the path we find another Occupation related memorial surrounded by low chains.

The **Deportees Memorial** is dedicated to those islanders forcibly removed from Jersey in September 1942 and sent to internment camps in Germany. The act was a reprisal ordered by Hitler in response to the British interring German citizens in Iran. With little notice, more than a thousand islanders with links to Britain through place of birth or residence had to leave, transported in ships to France and then on to camps in the south of Germany. Although once there conditions were not overly harsh, a number nevertheless died of ill health or other natural causes and are remembered to this day in annual ceremonies.

Follow one of the many paths through the magnificent park, making our way towards its main entrance marked out by the huge flagpole and bronze statue of King George V. On one side of the statue there is a somewhat ornate building partly obscured by foliage named the **Howard Davis Memorial Hall**, in which we find the reason for the park's existence. Howard Davis was the son of Thomas, or T.B., Davis, a Jersey-born, self-made millionaire, avid sailor and close friend of King George V. During the First World War, Howard served in the British Army and died of wounds received during the 1916 Battle of the Somme. After the war, his father established a number of scholarships and institutions as memorials to his son Howard, including this park, which he bought in 1937.

Leave the park via its main gate and turn left to follow La Colomberie as far as the pedestrian crossing. Turn left here into Green Street, passing the entrance of Green Street Cemetery and some public toilets before reaching the sloping entrance to the multi-storey car park. Cross the busy road here and take the steeply rising Regent Road until reaching a small bridge that we cross. Pause for a moment on the bridge to consider the cutting on the right, now a car park but formerly the railway terminus for the Jersey Eastern Railway, and originally quarried out to create a **massive defensive ditch for Fort Regent** that sits on the hill above. The walls of the fort's outer works are on our right as we continue along the quiet Rue de l'Est. At the time of the fort's construction in 1806, the land now occupied by houses to our left was open ground, and remained so for many years to create a clear field of fire from the fort to the seashore at Havre Des Pas. At the top of the road we reach Mount Bingham once more, and the starting point of our walk. Before the end, however, cross the road to inspect the memorial found at the entrance of the learner driver reversing bays.

Up until the summer of 1944, the few Allied airmen or sailors captured by the Germans in the island were transferred for imprisonment on the Continent. With the island cut off following the Allied invasion of France, this practice had to cease; the Germans at first held prisoners locally using the former British military prison at South Hill at first and then, as the numbers grew, created a purpose-built **South Hill Prisoner of War Camp** facility. The first inmates were nineteen Americans, wounded men captured during the fighting in France and sent to hospital in St Malo before their transfer to Jersey. In March 1945, 19 Americans captured in a German raid launched from Jersey against the small French port of Granville joined them, together with a small number of British taken at the same time. Fortunately, the end of the war was only weeks away, so their time spent in Jersey was a relatively short one.

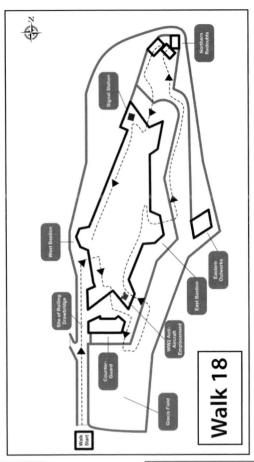

Walk 18

Walk Start

Site of Rolling Drawbridge

West Bastion

Signal Station

Northern Redoubts

Eastern Outworks

East Bastion

WW2 Anti-Aircraft Emplacement

Counter-Guard

Glacis Field

N

Above: The blend of old and new is seen throughout the fort

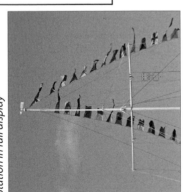

Below: Flags on the former Signal Station in full display

Walk 18: Commanding Views

A ramble around the ramparts of Fort Regent taking in its remarkable history, architecture and views

The massive ramparts of Fort Regent have dominated St Helier since its construction started in 1806 at the height of the Napoleonic Wars. The fact that, shortly after its completion, those wars ended meant it never had to defend the island in the manner intended, although its presence was certainly a deterrent against any attack. Following a government decision in 1967, the fort was transformed into a sports and leisure centre, although the value of doing so has dogged its reputation ever since. On this walk, we certainly discover Fort Regent's value in the form of a magnificent fortification, capped by remarkable modern architecture along with some of the most spectacular views in Jersey.

Start:	Mount Bingham Car Park
Length:	1.5 miles / 1.5 hours
Difficulty:	Moderate, with some slopes and steps to climb and descend
Getting there –	
By car:	Disc and scratch card parking at Mount Bingham or in Pier Road Car Park
By bus:	The start is within walking distance of Liberation Station
Refreshments:	A café inside the fort
Amenities:	Public toilets inside the fort

We start in the small car park above the children's playground on Mount Bingham, from where we can view the grass slope opposite that stretches up to a now derelict swimming pool building. While this 'Glacis Field' may appear a recent landscaping feature, it is in fact an integral part of the fort's defences, laid out at the time of its construction. With three sides of the fort protected by steep cliffs, this appears to be the most straightforward place for attack. It was a deception, however, designed to force an enemy into the open and expose them to the fire of cannon and infantry located at the top of the slope. Although it was never attempted, imagine for a moment what it would have been like to march up Glacis Field in the face of cannon and musket fire knowing that on this open ground there was nowhere to hide.

There is no public entrance to the fort from the Glacis Field today, so we take the main access road, which starts opposite Mount Bingham Car Park, noting the commanding views over St Helier and St Aubin's Bay as we climb higher. Shortly after a road on the left leads to the top of Pier Road Car Park, a row of **rusting spikes** appears on top of the wall on the same side. While they may look like the sad remains of an earlier decorative finish, their positioning here is deliberate and relates to the fort's former defences. To hinder any attempt to reach the fort's entrance using this original access road, a ditch, or dry moat, blocked the way at this point. The spikes prevented anyone attempting to get round by climbing on top of the wall, while from the opposite side a **rolling drawbridge** came out from beneath the rampart there to span the moat and provide access for those allowed to pass.

Continue up the access road until reaching the modern-day lift shaft on the left, which is a good place to stop to consider the fort's role and design. Fort Regent, named after the then Prince Regent, was built between 1806 and 1814 as the island's principal fortification, taking over from Elizabeth Castle that lies outside the harbour below. Its powerful cannon, emplaced on top of the walls or in casemates at various locations, protected the town and harbour from enemy attack, either by warship or from an invasion force landing elsewhere and advancing across country. Yet the fort was only part of a far larger defensive system, built after the French invasion of 1781 proved how vulnerable Jersey was. Around the coast, a network of towers and batteries, as well as older fortifications, formed a first line of defence against invasion, while barracks around the island held troops ready to move by a network of military roads to wherever the enemy landed. At the hub of these defences was Fort Regent, providing support for local forces fighting on the coast or inland, or as a stronghold to hold out until the arrival of a relieving British fleet. The plans were never tested, of course, but given its strength of position and design, it would surely have done an excellent job.

The design of the fort reflected the latest features of the day. Dressed granite walls, such the one in front us, were 18-feet thick to absorb bombardment and pierced by embrasures through which cannon could return fire. At the corners of the fort and jutting out from the sides are angled bastions and redans, from which smaller cannons and muskets could create a killing field for any attackers attempting to reach the walls. Standing here at the lift and looking at the fort, jutting out on the right is the 'South-west Redan' while the 'West Bastion' protrudes on the left, with an entrance leading inside complete with keystone engraved 1806. This is not an original stone or entrance, however, having been constructed in recent years to allow vehicle access to the interior of the fort. The original gate lies behind the modern-day entrance building, through which we go to enter the fort. Just before doing so, however, note that in front of the West Bastion is a set of original steps, allowing the garrison easier access between the fort and town. Until recent years a public house that stood quite near to the foot of these steps was called the 'First and Last', signifying the soldiers first and last place for a drink on a night out.

Passing through the modern entrance building we walk up the gently sloping access tunnel, noting the plaque on the wall recalling this being the last posting for the Jersey Militia before their departure for overseas service in June 1940, and another explaining the Neolithic dolmen found here when construction started in 1806. Note also the extraordinary detail of the block work on the ceiling, a feature found throughout the fort that denotes the skill that went into its building at a time when virtually all work was done by hand.

All manner of buildings and partitions fill the interior of the fort today, making it difficult to envisage the whole area now under the roof as a spacious open parade ground, but for most of its existence, it was just that. The rooms found today in the walls around the edge were once **military offices, barracks, storerooms,** etc., and filled with soldiers going about their day-to-day duties. During the Occupation, another group filled this area as the Germans used the barrack rooms to house workers brought to Jersey to build the fortifications. At first **Lager Ehrenbreitstein** housed political prisoners, but after 1941

Plaque inside the main entrance tunnel recalling the last duties of the Jersey Militia

they left to make way for French North African forced labourers, some of whom may have stayed here until the end of the Occupation.

Before moving on, step away from the entrance to view the fort's **foundation stone** above, giving the name of the man who commissioned it, General Don, then the island's lieutenant-governor, and its designer, Lieutenant-Colonel John Humfrey.

Turn right from the entrance, following the interior wall around behind the children's play area until reaching another smaller tunnel marked exit that takes us outside of the fort once more. Here we are in one of the '**ditches**', a sort of dry moat surrounding the fort proper and again covered by fire from several angles. Note that the walls on one side of the ditch have smooth and meticulously set dressed granite blocks, while in other places there is a far more rudimentary finish. The reason for this is that only those walls likely to face bombardment by an enemy needed the dressed granite to improve their ability to absorb and deflect fire. Elsewhere, in less exposed places, the simpler (and cheaper) construction suffices.

Turn left here, going further into the fort, before turning right to climb the slope and steps leading up to the old swimming pool. Although the buildings and walls here make it impossible to see, we are now at the top of the Glacis Field and standing among a series of cleverly designed and multi-layered defences. To understand how they worked, turn left onto the landscaped path running on top of the walls here before stopping to overlook the ditch. Between the top of the Glacis Field and the first rampart, there is a ditch, which attackers would have had to cross. The first rampart is part of a detached fortification called the 'Counter-guard', from which cannon and infantry could have fired down the slope at attacking troops. Between the Counter-guard and the fort's South-east Redan is another ditch, which again needed crossing. Note that the South-east Redan is higher than the Counter-guard, while in turn the Counter-Guard is higher than the top of Glacis Field, a multi-level arrangement allowing both to sweep the Glacis Field with fire.

Walking away from the pool building, follow the wooded path for a short distance before taking the bridge on the left to cross the ditch and then climb the steps to reach the South-east Redan, noting a small plaque on the right commemorating the erection of this and other bridges by members of the British Army in 1968. Inside the redan there are steps on the left leading up to a concrete anti-aircraft emplacement. The only time guns on Fort Regent ever fired in anger was during the Occupation, when the Germans placed three 2cm anti-aircraft guns here in emplacements like this one. They opened fire several times, gaining the dubious record of shooting down a German plane passing over the island in April 1944, killing all four members of its crew.

Leaving the emplacement, which was built on top of an earlier British gun position, walk towards the glass and steel wall and roof and turn right to follow the wide walkway here. After a short distance, an exit sign points right and a path takes us to the interior of the East Bastion, today a pretty but infrequently visited rose garden. Note the granite sets and emplacements that once housed multiple cannons here, before crossing the bridge over the ditch to reach the Eastern Outer Ramparts, and their pleasant path that, after turning left, we follow taking in the magnificent views of eastern St Helier and St Clement.

Despite the commanding views, the designers of the fort considered this eastern side its weakest, taking great care to increase the level and complexity of fortifications. Firstly, quarrying and

A bricked-up embrasure in the East Bastion, once housing a cannon that would have dominated the fort's eastern approaches

digging helped isolate the fort from the ground below by creating a massive ditch in which Snow Hill Car Park now stands. Secondly, there was the outer rampart on which we are now standing, which needed capturing before any attack on the fort itself from this direction. Visible below and on the right as we walk along is the final piece of insurance, an additional detached fortification called the **Eastern Outworks** constructed on the rocky spur that today overlooks the eastern entrance to the road tunnel passing under the fort. These outworks, which are no longer open to the public, featured more ditches and cannon emplacements together with further rolling bridges to restrict access. They are also the site of a now closed and derelict cable car station that once brought visitors up from town below.

Continuing on, the rampart walk opens out into an area called the **Northern Redoubts**, today mostly filled by the forlorn remains of a mini-golf course and some attractive gardens. The redoubts themselves – redoubt meaning an enclosed defensive emplacement outside a larger fort – are actually on a lower level, accessible through a gate located in the right-hand corner of this area, although often locked unless a special request is made. To reach it we pass the probable remains of a **mortar battery**, and a huge vent pipe from a storm-water management system constructed in recent years far below. The redoubts once housed cannon to protect the fort's eastern flank and fire against anyone approaching from the south-west. Today, although the cannon are long gone, marvellous views remain, particular over town which is now close enough to remind us how near it is to Fort Regent.

Leaving the redoubts, walk through the rose gardens, taking time to admire yet more stunning views over St Helier. Cross the bridge leading over the ditch to enter the fort proper once again, arriving in the North-east Redan, Here we find a large gun emplacement, constructed in concrete and probably dating to the mid or late 19th century. A path from here leads to the **North-west Redan**, today filled by the former **signal station** and a forest of mobile phone masts and other communication apparatus.

There was a signal station here on Le Mont de la Ville prior to the construction of the fort, one of ten established in late 18th century to relay information on shipping movements, especially those which involved French warships that may have been approaching the island. The network continued to function throughout the 19th century, although used increasingly for commercial purposes, relaying information on the approach of merchant ships and their cargoes. During the Occupation, when the Germans garrisoned the fort, a swastika flag flew here. One of the first acts of the liberating forces in May 1945 being to march up and haul it down, before hoisting the British flag in its place. In 2004, after the Harbour Department ceased formally flying flags, volunteers from Jersey Heritage took over to continue providing the striking displays enjoyed from the town and harbour below.

Linking the North-west Redan to West Bastion, which was badly damaged during the 1970's development, are the **Western Ramparts**, which our walk follows next. Although an attack from this direction was extremely unlikely given the terrain, the huge outer wall here is nevertheless 18-feet thick to protect against enemy bombardment. We pass several **embrasures for the cannon** once mounted here, although development to improve access and viewing has removed others and the earth parapet that once covered much of the top. Perhaps the changes are worth it for the view, which as we reach the main viewing platform, is a spectacular one over the harbour, waterfront and beyond to Elizabeth Castle. It leaves little doubt as to the commanding views granted to any defender here, and the challenge faced by any attacker considering their options to take the fort.

As our walk finishes and we make our way back inside to reach the main gate, think about which role you would rather have played – attacker or defender?

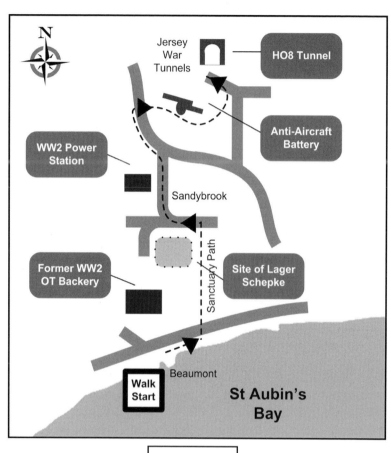

Walk 19

Walk 19: No Sanctuary

An inland walk that follows a former sanctuary path to visit a once forgotten anti-aircraft battery and the most famous tunnel in Jersey.

There is a story that fugitives who reached one of Jersey's parish churches in ancient times could find sanctuary there, and along a path leading to the sea by which they could escape the island. How much truth there is in this remains open to speculation, but here and there, these so-called sanctuary paths remain as part of the landscape. This walk starts by following one to pass the site a camp used during the Occupation for housing the slave labourers brought to the island to construct the fortifications. For its inmates, the path offered no sanctuary, instead taking them to some of the island's harshest and most dangerous construction projects, among them the tunnel complex now home to the Jersey War Tunnels.

Start:	Outside the Gunsite Café at Beaumont
Length:	1.5 miles / 1.5 hours
Difficulty:	Moderate, with one steep path to climb and descend
Getting there –	
By car:	Chargeable parking at Beaumont
By bus:	Routes 12 and 15 from Liberation Station, alighting at Beaumont
Refreshments:	Gunsite Café near the start and Jersey War Tunnels Café at the end
Amenities:	Toilets at Beaumont and the Jersey War Tunnels

From the café, which is a German bunker covered on Walk 2, follow the coastal walk back towards St Helier until reaching a small car park about two hundred metres away. Cross the main road here using the pedestrian crossing and take the footpath that leads inland. This track is believed to be the final section of an ancient sanctuary or 'perquage' path running from St Lawrence Church to the sea, a route taken by fugitives wishing to escape Jersey and any crimes they may be accused of. Although there is little historical evidence to support the existence of sanctuary paths, that hasn't stopped this path going by that name for as long as people can remember.

A short distance after starting on the path, another branches left towards a car park overlooked by a large concrete structure. Built during the Occupation, this was originally a bake house producing bread for the workforce of labourers brought to the island to build the German fortifications. Nearby, visible across the field to the left, was **Lager Schepke,** one of the camps used to house some of that workforce and today the site of a number of small industrial units.

The former Organisation Todt bake house at Beaumont, now a warehouse and sports shop

During the Occupation, the Germans brought several thousand workers to Jersey to build the fortifications. Their backgrounds prior to arriving, and the treatment received once here, varied. Some were Western Europeans who worked for the Germans as volunteers or conscripts, and received pay, accommodation and reasonable living and working conditions in exchange. Others came as forced labourers, including French North Africans and Spanish Republicans handed over by the pro-Nazi French Vichy regime to work for the Germans. While their conditions of work and living were poor, they were at least better than those received by workers in the final category. The slave labourers working in Jersey came mostly from Eastern Europe - Russians, Ukrainians and other nationalities rounded up, or captured as prisoners-of-war, and sent west to work for Germany.

During the Occupation, Lager Schepke housed a mix of Russians and Spaniards who worked on the German tunnels being built to house ammunition, supplies and other stores in St Peter's Valley and Beaumont Valley. They laboured underground for long hours, blasting and digging galleries out of the rock, a task not only extremely arduous but also fraught with danger from tunnel collapses. Poorly fed and clothed, local residents can still recall these workers shuffling along the route we take on this walk, pitifully begging for any scraps of food. Spare these poor wretches a thought as we continue on our way.

The 'sanctuary path' ends at Sandybrook, where we turn left and then right into La Rue du Moulin de Tesson, continuing for about three hundred metres until reaching a large white building on the left. Today used as part of a garage workshop, it actually dates from the Occupation when its purpose was to help provide the electricity required to power the vast fortification construction programme then going on. This high demand for electricity brought the Germans into conflict with

Now a motor workshop, the Germans constructed this building during the Occupation as a power station

179

the island's authorities whose prime concern was ensuring civilian electricity needs. As the island's power station, then at Queen's Road, used diesel as a fuel, the Germans decided to build a **coal-fired power station**, and work started here in 1942. Steam-powered generators were brought to the island, and installed in the four bays visible at the front of this building. In the end, it was something of a futile exercise, as the German fortification programme was running down as this power station came on line, and both diesel and coal ran out after supplies from France ceased during the final winter of the war.

Walking on, we pass **Tesson Mill**, a large granite-faced building that played an important role in feeding the civilian population during the Occupation. Arriving at the main road through St Peter's Valley, we turn left onto the footpath running alongside. After a short distance, there is the entrance to a footpath on the opposite side of the road, which we take, climbing up through the trees until reaching the top, where we pause for a moment.

Given the thickness of tree cover now found here, it is difficult to believe that the whole site was open during the Occupation, and the location of a powerful German heavy **anti-aircraft battery** armed with six 8.8cm and three 2cm anti-aircraft guns. The location here at Les Gellettes was carefully chosen, situated close to the flight path for planes approaching the airport from the east, and with views over St Aubin's Bay where our walk started. As such, it could not only engage Allied aircraft, but also provide artillery support for the island's nearby coastal defences. After the Occupation, the weapons and ammunition were removed, and most of the site reverted to farmland. But in the area near the front of the hill, woods were allowed to grow and cover parts of the former battery, leaving the remains of bunkers, trenches and barbed wire concealed in the undergrowth. In recent years, however, the battery was 'rediscovered', with the site partially cleared to allow access. Then, in 2011, a visit by Channel Four's Time Team firmly secured its status as a place of interest as they carried out one of their popular three-day archaeological digs on the site, uncovering formerly buried features and generally reinterpreting what happened here in the war.

Our visit starts by taking the path straight ahead. After a short distance, the well-defined remains of a **shallow German trench** appear on the right, winding through the trees to cross the path and continue into the undergrowth. Many of these narrow trenches, which run all across and around the site, were dug in 1944 to provide the battery with all-round defence against a ground attack and to offer a second line of defence against any attempt to advance inland through the valley below.

Six of these fearsome 8.8cm guns were installed in a formerly 'lost' battery on high ground above St Peter's Valley (CIOS Collection)

Crossing the trench, continue on the main path, passing another trench that leads away to a **small bunker** on the right. Note that this is a very rudimentary structure compared to bunkers elsewhere, but its role and those of others on this site was to offer basic protection for the gun crews and a location to store ammunition. Returning to the main path, continue until reaching a fork to the left, alongside which there is a felled tree stump. Follow this side path until reaching a second bunker with a path behind leading through the undergrowth to a **large concrete platform.** This was once the mounting for one of the battery's fearsome 8.8cm anti-aircraft guns.

The German 8.8cm gun acquired a formidable reputation during the Second World War, both as an anti-aircraft gun and in its ground role against Allied tanks and infantry targets. When firing at aircraft, it had a range of up to 10,600 metres, using a powerful range finder to locate and track targets. In these peaceful woods today, it is hard to imagine the noise and concussion of all six guns firing at once or the potentially devastating consequences for those in the planes flying above.

Returning to the bunker, take the path leading off to the right that skirts the fields, under which many remains of the battery, including its command and control post lie to this day. On the right of the path, we pass various earthworks denoting former structures and emplacements before arriving at an open rectangular space surrounded on three sides by earth banks. This was one of the sites excavated by Time Team, who concluded from finds that it was the location of the battery's ablutions block, a wooden hut used by its soldiers for washing and cleaning. Alongside, we find a round concrete object, possibly a water butt to collect run-off from the roof.

Leaving this area, we follow the small path away that eventually re-unites with the main path running through the site. While our walk goes left passing further concrete installations to descend to the road below, we could spend more time exploring the whole site.

An ex-French tank turret installed outside the Jersey War Tunnels, today the island's foremost visitor attraction

After arriving at the road, turn left to walk up to the Jersey War Tunnels. Work on the tunnel here started in 1941, with the intention of constructing a vast underground artillery servicing and repair complex, designated HO8 (*HO standing for Hohlgangsanlagen, or cave passage installation*). By 1944, however, with the tunnel complex still not complete, the Germans decided to convert it into a casualty receiving station equipped with wards and an operating theatre. Although it was never actually used as such, the name 'German Underground Hospital' stuck after the Occupation when the tunnel became a visitor attraction in the 1950s. In 2003, there was a change of direction with a new name of Jersey War Tunnels and new exhibitions focusing on Jersey's experience during the Second World War rather than just the role of this tunnel. The substantial investment has been justly rewarded, with the site remaining among the most popular visitor attractions in the island.

Along with the new identity, came an archive facility next to the car park focused on the Occupation. Outside is an ex-French tank turret recovered from one of the island's bunkers. A new visitor centre and café was also provided, in which we can take a welcome break at the end of our walk before returning to its start at Beaumont by following the road leading to the War Tunnels until it reaches the main road through St Peter's Valley which we cross to re-enter La Rue du Moulin de Tesson. Alternatively, take the bus from the War Tunnels back to St Helier

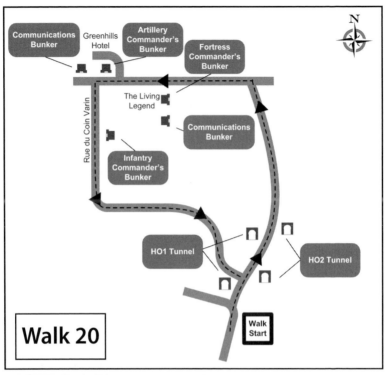

Walk 20

The lower entrance to HO1, today a controlled storage facility

Walk 20: At the Heart of Things

A short circular walk around quiet country roads and lanes to visit German tunnels and command bunkers.

In contrast to all others in the book, this walk neither starts nor finishes on the coast, taking us instead deep into the island's quiet and leafy heartland. While the majority of Jersey's German fortifications are understandably sited along its coastline, they were only the hardened outer shell of a fortress that encompassed the whole island. On this walk, we discover the heart of this fortress, a massive command and communications complex responsible for controlling the island's defences. We also visit some of the vital underground ammunition and supply storage facilities for the fortress, found now in a sleepy little valley with a dark past from both the Occupation and the years that followed.

Start:	Outside the Victoria in the Valley pub
Length:	2 miles / 1.5 hours
Difficulty:	Easy, with only gentle climbs and descents
Getting there:	
By car:	Limited but car park available for patrons of the pub
By bus:	Route 8 from Liberation Station, alighting at the Victoria in the Valley pub
Refreshments:	Food and refreshment options at the start, end and en route
Amenities:	Toilets located in places of refreshment

At the side of the pub, take the road called La Route de l'Aleval, or unofficially, 'the German Road'. Although the route up this valley was just a small country track prior to the Occupation, work started here in 1941 that soon transformed this formerly quiet branch of St Peter's Valley into the centre of a massive construction project. And it was all due to an order from Adolf Hitler that the island must be have secure accommodation for stores and ammunition.

In setting out his expectations for Jersey's conversion to an impregnable fortress, Hitler highlighted the need to ensure the garrison had the right facilities for holding the supplies necessary to withstand a siege or defeat an enemy attack. The solution arrived at was a series of massive tunnel complexes, bored into the sides of Jersey's valleys and hillsides at suitable locations. This little valley was chosen for two, and possibly three, of the largest.

After a short walk up the road, we arrive at the first one. Next to the small house on the left hand side is the **lower entrance of HO1,** (*HO standing for Hohlgangsanlage or cave passage installation*), an extensive tunnel complex built for the storage of ammunition that extends back into the hillside along the lower part of the valley. Workers from the German State Labour Service started its construction in 1941, with their crossed-hammer emblem and the dates 41-42 visible on the keystone above this entrance. The complex was planned to hold 20,000 tons of supplies in its extensive galleries, although it was never fully completed. After the Occupation, the British Army placed many of the smaller German weapons inside and sealed the entrances, only for it to be reopened a few years later so they could be retrieved for scrap. The tunnel then passed into private hands, becoming a mushroom farm for many years, before a recent transformation to a controlled storage facility.

On the opposite side of the valley, there is the **second tunnel complex, designated HO2,** built mostly by Russian and French North African labourers for the storage of rations. Unlike HO1, its front galleries were never fully completed, leaving rough rock-hewn entrances such as the one found among the foliage a little further up the valley. Also in contrast to HO1, the contents of this tunnel complex were not removed in the 1950s scrap drive, leaving tons of former German Army equipment rusting behind its sealed entrances, including thousands of soldier's helmets. The lure of this military hardware proved irresistible to collectors and souvenir hunters, who gained access to HO2 by breaking a hole through the concrete seal on the tunnel entrance. But in 1962, tragedy struck after someone lit a fire in one of the galleries. Three boys entering the next day were overcome by the build-up of deadly carbon monoxide that resulted from the fire, with two of them losing their lives in the tunnel.

The upper entrance to HO2, showing the access hole cut into the concrete seal after the Occupation to gain access

Following this, the tunnel was cleared of most materials, although enough lingered to ensure a continued interest. During the 1980s, there was a further clearance and attempts to find a useful purpose for HO2, but the unfinished entrances and unlined internal galleries limited options. Today the tunnel remains derelict, an enigmatic testament to the labours of those who built it and those who lost their lives in pursuit of its contents.

Moving up the road, on the right-hand side we find a further reminder of German construction effort here in the form of the skeletal concrete remains of a **stone crusher,** used to create the aggregate needed for the tunnel's concrete wall linings. Opposite on the other side of the valley is a **second entrance for HO1,** this one a smaller personnel entrance, while a little way further on the same side is the **upper entrance of HO1,** complete with air-pumping machinery as a legacy of its mushroom growing days. The reason for having upper and lower entrances was to allow vehicle access into the tunnel and then out again after loading or unloading.

On the opposite side, we find the **upper entrance of HO2,** which, like the lower one, is unlined and incomplete. Approaching it does give an idea of the massive scale of construction work undertaken during the Occupation, mostly by forced and slave labourers toiling in harsh and unforgiving conditions. The hole seen in the post-war concrete seal also shows the effort made to gain access to the tunnel after the Occupation, a determination that would lead to the loss of two young lives.

Leaving the tunnels behind, we continue our walk up the valley, which climbs gently before opening out into countryside. Rumours abound that somewhere in the upper area of the valley there is another tunnel complex, this one a huge **personnel shelter designated HO6**, although nothing has ever been found other than a reference in wartime reports. Upon reaching the top of the road, turn left and, taking care given its narrow nature, walk along until reaching a house on the left hand side called 'Maison l'Aleval', just after which there is a grit track. We are now within the perimeter of the German's fortress command and communication complex, which controlled the island's defences during the Occupation.

The *Kernwerk (Kern meaning heart or core)* was built after August 1942 to provide a secure and fortified battle headquarters for the island's military commanders. Its most important components were five massive concrete bunkers, three of which were two-storey constructions complete with washrooms, flushing toilets and central heating. Also part of the complex was a water pumping and storage bunker and anti-aircraft positions (the concrete gun mountings for these are found in a field boundary behind the Greenhills Hotel). Underground telephone links connected the bunkers here with those around the island, while direct lines also linked Kernwerk to Guernsey, Paris and, through the latter, to Berlin. For many years, the **Fortress Commander bunker**, which is located to the right near the start of this track, was open to the public as part of the tourist complex that is today the Living Legend. It is now hidden among the buildings here, and no longer publically accessible. A little further along this track, however, on the right hand side there is an associated **communications bunker**.

Coming back to the tarmac road, carry on past the entrance to the Living Legend (under threat of development at the time of writing) on the left and the Greenhills Hotel, just to the right, both of which serve refreshments. Passing the Living Legend, walk the short distance to a junction with the Rue du Coin Varin, which turns left, and Le Mont de St Anastase, which goes straight ahead. Look carefully at the property opposite Rue du Coin Varin and notice that all is not as it seems. This house is built around the **Fortress Artillery Commander bunker**, another of the huge two-storey constructions, while a short distance further along Le Mont de St Anastase there is another **communications bunker** on the same side and again used today as part of a private home.

Coming back to the junction, we take Rue du Coin Varin, walking for about 300 metres to find the final *Kernwerk* bunker in a field on the left, this one the **Fortress Infantry Commander bunker**. Without

The impressive Fortress Infantry Commander bunker on Rue du Coin Varin, complete with false window and chimneys and today the most readily visible fortification of Kernwerk

other constructions or foliage to obscure it, the size, design and build of these impressive installations become obvious. They were built to resemble houses, with false chimney pots and windows on each end, including shutters built to complete the effect. The two entrance doors, which would have been protected by a small moat, still have their grills in place, while watching over them is an **entrance defence loophole**. Even in its current state of repair, the bunker remains a hugely impressive and somewhat menacing symbol of efforts made by the Germans to turn Jersey into a fortress par excellence.

Leaving the bunker behind, our walk continues along Rue du Coin Varin, which offers sumptuous views over the neighbouring valley and the island's south coast beyond, and then straight into Rue du Panigot, which eventually winds back down to end near the Victoria in the Valley pub where our walk started.

Enfin

All books should have a conclusion and this one is no exception. Here I would like to record my thanks to those who helped in the writing and preparation of this book, and those whose invaluable preceding work helped make it possible. Among the latter are Michael Ginns, MBE and his majestic book Jersey Occupied: The German Armed Forces in Jersey 1940-1945. Also in this category is William Davies who wrote a History of Fort Regent and The Coastal Towers of Jersey, both of which were useful sources of information. For the use of certain photos, special thanks must also go to the Société Jersiaise and the Channel Islands Occupation Society, about whom further information can be found at www.ciosjersey.org.uk and thanks to Paul Sewell for generously contributing the front cover image.

Another website to draw to the attention of readers is the one that accompanies this book, www.jerseywarwalks.com. While its principal purpose is to further the knowledge of Jersey's outstanding range of fortifications and fascinating military history, this website is also the place to submit feedback on the experience of reading and using this book and walking the walks. What would you have added or taken away to improve things, for example, or what worked well and what disappointed? Who knows, if there is a further reprint, your feedback might just help improve things for someone else.

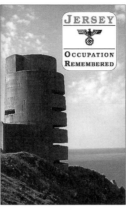

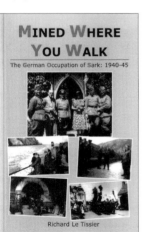
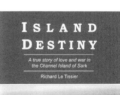

Complete list of Seaflower Books, 2016:

BLAME THE BADGER by Mike Stentiford OBE	£6.95
CHANNEL FISH by Marguerite Paul	£11.95
EXOTIC GARDEN PLANTS IN THE CHANNEL ISLANDS by Janine Le Pivert	£9.95
A FARMER'S VACATION IN 1873 by George E Waring	£5.00
GUERNSEY COUNTRY DIARY by Nigel Jee	£4.95
ISLAND DESTINY by Richard Le Tissier	£6.95
ISLAND KITCHEN by Marguerite Paul	£11.95
JERSEY HORSES FROM THE PAST by John Jean	£4.95
JERSEY IN LONDON by Brian Ahier Read	£6.95
JERSEY JAUNTS by John Le Dain	£6.95
THE JERSEY LILY by Sonia Hillsdon	£6.95
JERSEY OCCUPATION DIARY by Nan Le Ruez	£9.95
JERSEY OCCUPATION REMEMBERED by Sonia Hillsdon	£5.95
JERSEY RAMBLES by John Le Dain	£6.95
JERSEY: THE HIDDEN HISTORIES by Paul Darroch	£9.95
JERSEY WEATHER AND TIDES by Peter Manton	£5.95
JERSEY WITCHES, GHOSTS & TRADITIONS by Sonia Hillsdon	£6.95
JOHN SKINNER'S VISIT TO THE CHANNEL ISLANDS: August 1827	£2.50
JOURNEY ACROSS JERSEY by Robin Pittman	£5.95
JOURNEY ROUND JERSEY by Robin Pittman	£7.95
JOURNEY ROUND ST HELIER by Robin Pittman	£7.95
LA CHAIRE by Stephen Harmer	£6.95
LIFE ON SARK by Jennifer Cochrane	£5.95
LOW WATER FISHING by David Le Maistre	£6.95
MINED WHERE YOU WALK by Richard Le Tissier	£6.95
THE POOR SHALL INHERIT Daff Noel	£6.95
PRISON WITHOUT BARS by Frank Keiller	£6.95
WILD ISLAND by Peter Double	£7.95
WILDLIFE OF THE CHANNEL ISLANDS by Sue Daly	£14.95
WISH YOU WERE HERE by John Le Dain	£7.95

Please visit our website for more details: **www.ex-librisbooks.co.uk**
SEAFLOWER BOOKS may be ordered through our website using Paypal
We send books post-free within the UK and Channel Islands
SEAFLOWER BOOKS are also available via your local bookshop
or from Amazon.com